the Idler

ISSUE 35 | SPRING 2005

First published in Great Britain in 2005

10 9 8 7 6 5 4 3 2 1

The Idler, Issue 35
© copyright Idle Limited, 2005

First published by Ebury Press, Random House, 20 Vauxhall Bridge
Road, London SW1V 2SA

Random House Australia (Pty) Limited
20 Alfred Street, Milsons Point, Sydney, New South Wales 2061, Australia
Random House New Zealand Limited
18 Poland Road, Glenfield, Auckland 10, New Zealand
Random House South Africa (Pty) Limited
Endulini, 5A Jubilee Road, Parktown 2193, South Africa
The Random House Group Limited Reg. No. 954009
www.randomhouse.co.uk
A CIP catalogue record for this book is available from the British Library.
Cover Design by Vince
Text design and typesetting by Sonia Ortiz Alcón

ISBN 0091905125

Papers used by Ebury Press are natural, recyclable products made from
wood grown in sustainable forests.

Printed and bound in Germany by Appl, Wemding

Editor: Tom Hodgkinson   **Creative Director:** Gavin Pretor-Pinney
Deputy Editor: Dan Kieran   **Editor at Large:** Matthew De Abaitua
Designer: Sonia Ortiz Alcón   **Managing Editor:** Edward Sage
Advertising and Promotional Director: Will Hogan
Literary Editor: Tony White   **Music Editor:** Will Hodgkinson
Contributing Editors: Greg Rowland, Ian Vince
Advertising: Jamie Dwelly at Cabbell 020 8971 8450
For editorial enquiries call 020 7691 0320

What is **the Idler**?

The Idler is a magazine that celebrates
freedom, fun and the fine art
of doing nothing.

We believe that idleness is unjustly
criticized in modern society when it is,
in fact, a vital component of a happy life.

We want to comfort and inspire you with
uplifting philosophy, satire and
reflection, as well as giving
practical information to help in the quest
for the idle life.

www.independentrecordsltd.com
info@independentrecordsltd.com

irl023
sharon shannon
tunes

all titles available on amazon.co.uk

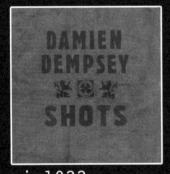

irl022
damien dempsey
shots

irl021
siobhan parr
lose my dress

irl020
the wonder stuff
escape from rubbish island

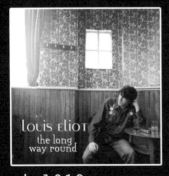

irl019
louis eliot
the long way round

irl018
damien dempsey
seize the day

irl014
tinariwen
amassakoul

HANNAH DYSON

CHRIS DONALD P24

Contents THE IDLER, ISSUE 35, SPRING 2005

8 EDITOR'S LETTER
10 NOTES ON CONTRIBUTORS

··

NOTES FROM THE COUCH

14 IDLER'S DIARY
16 READERS' LETTERS
20 SKIVERS AND STRIVERS
22 TONY HUSBAND'S JOKES PAGE
23 THE FINE LINE BETWEEN MICE AND MEN
24 CHRIS DONALD ON THE TOILET
28 ADAM BUXTON PRESENTS KEN KORDA
30 THE VEGAN CHINESE
34 RUBEN MORGAN: ACTING IS FOR IDLERS
36 THE EVENING STROLLERS' SOCIETY
38 THE TRUTH: BRIAN DEAN HAS SOME
     STATISTICS ABOUT THE HORRORS OF
     WORK
42 ROWLEY LEIGH IS THE IDLE COOK
43 LIBRARY OF THE MONTH: THE MARX
     MEMORIAL LIBRARY
44 THE WIT AND WISDOM OF AUBERON
     WAUGH
48 MORE FORMS FROM IAN VINCE
52 QUESTIONNAIRE: TERRY HALL
54 THE STORY OF MASQUERADE
58 QUIZ SHOWS RANKED BY CLASS

60 CRAP HOLIDAYS: FINDHORN
61 IDLE PLEASURES: SUNBEAMS
62 UNIVERSITY OF IDLERS
64 CRAP HOLIDAYS: EGYPT
67 NEVILLE BY TONY HUSBAND
71 QUESTIONNAIRE: NICK BROOMFIELD
72 FROM THE PEN OF PETER DOHERTY:
     BEING LEGS AND LOOPBILO
74 FISHHEADS BY PETE LOVEDAY
76 BILL AND ZED'S BAD ADVICE

··

CONVERSATIONS

80 RAOUL VANEIGEM Laurence Remila
     meets the great situationist
     philosopher

··

FEATURES

90 KEITH ALLEN'S A-TO-Z OF LIFE
     Featuring Keith's "Naked" 2005 Tsunami
     Appeal Calendar
100 THE STORY OF ROBERT BLINCOE
     Was Nicholas Blincoe's rabble-rousing
     ancestor the model for Oliver Twist?
106 FOLK ART
     Jeremy Deller and ALAN KANE present
     art by the people

BARTENDER,
THERE'S *CUCUMBER* IN MY GIN.

Fear not, all the surprises of this gin taste marvelous. **HENDRICK'S®** *is instilled with juniper, coriander, citrus peel and a particularly luscious infusion of rose petal and* **cucumber**.

Hendrick's Gin is avaialable at Harvey Nichols, Peckhams (Scotland), Gerry's of Old Compton Street, drinkon.com, Lea & Sandemann, thewhiskyexchange.com and other unusual retailers.

HENDRICK'S
A MOST UNUSUAL GIN

HENDRICKSGIN.COM

JEFF HARRISON

THE IDLER ABROAD P206

More Contents
THE IDLER, ISSUE 35, SPRING 2005

120 WAR ON THE WORKSHY
Jack Thurston accuses New Labour of
attacking idlers

126 WAR NOT WORK
Richard Donkin recalls the warriors of
old who preferred fighting to toiling

132 PLAY AWAY
Pat Kane attacks Will Hutton's dull and
tedious Work Foundation

138 LITERARY LOAFERS
We study the great dawdlers of
literature

146 SLACKING ALL OVER THE WORLD
Edward Sage on the anti-work
movements springing up across the
globe

STORIES
152 HARRY BRAVADO
Matthew De Abaitua's tale of a new job
in Canary Wharf

162 THE APPLICATION
BY Clare Pollard

THE PRACTICAL IDLER
171 THE SEVEN STEPS OF DAN KIERAN
Dan's guide to doing what you want

176 BRING ME MY ROD
Kevin Parr's goes fishing

179 NOTEBOOK OF THE MONTH
Celebrating the fabulous Moleskine

180 USEFUL THING: WD-40
Chris Yates on the wonderstuff

182 THE ART OF WAR
We meet top fencer Kirk Zavier

184 BUILD YOUR OWN SAUNA
Will Hogan goes back to the womb

186 HAPPY TEA
A miraculous blend to cure melancholy

188 THE PASSENGER
Fanny Johnstone on the Vauxhall Corsa

190 CIGARS
Tim Richardson gets befuddled

196 THE BROWSER: Geoff Dyer's bookshelf,
Jeff Lint and the Freedom Bookshop

200 MUSIC: An interview with DJ Unfit for
work and John Moore's guide to going
solo

206 THE IDLER ABROAD: CAMBODIA
Julian Watson escapes the work ethic

211 FILM: BRANDO: The Method and The
madness, Paul Hamilton hides his face
in despair

224 GREG ROWLAND's dreams come true

EDITOR'S LETTER

WELCOME to our War on Work issue. Why declare a war on work? Well, according to recent UN figures, work kills over two million people every year worldwide. That's more than war, it's more than drugs, it's more than alcohol. It's the equivalent to two 9/11s every day. Yet we see no War on Work being declared by the world's governments. And that's because work has become a religion. It has replaced salvation as the goal of human beings. The work-and-consume ethic has surpassed previous moralities which were based on cooperation and sharing. It has become the promise of life. But it's a promise that has failed to deliver and that's why we are declaring war on it.

But that's not to say that we can't redefine work. Creative work and work that is freely chosen can be a great pleasure. The idler finds that when he or she is engaged in activities that we control, we are actually capable of putting in quite a lot of effort. It's when the work is imposed on us by an outside agency that it becomes such a drag.

In this issue, former Labour Party advisor Jack Thurston attacks Westminster's obsession with the notion of hard-working families and argues for more humane policies when it comes to toil. Free spirits Keith Allen and Peter Doherty give us an insight into their minds, while Chris Donald and Alex James reflect on the pleasures of those idler's retreats, toilets and sheds.

We've also got some fantastic images from Jeremy Deller and Alan Kane's Folk Art Archive project, which celebrates the creativity of ordinary people.

We're also immensely privileged to feature a conversation with Raoul Vaneigem, who with Guy Debord was one of the outstanding situationist writers and activists of the 1960s. "Ne Travaillez Jamais" was one of their slogans and Vaneigem is still in fighting form.

So till the next time, let us live free and live well and begin to create an earthly paradise.

TOM HODGKINSON
tom@idler.co.uk

IDLER CONTRIBUTORS

Who are the idlers?

IAN Aitch is the inventor of World Phone in Sick Day and the author of *A Fête Worse Than Death – A Journey Through an English Summer*. He lives at www.iainaitch.com

Keith Allen is a grown-up

Marc Baines runs the Salty Cellar club in Glasgow

Adam Buxton is the comic genius who was part of Adam and Joe and is now filming his own films

Matthew De Abaitua is always available

Brian Dean runs the excellent website anxietyculture.com

Jeremy Deller won this year's Turner Prize. He is co-curator of Folk Art with Alan Kane

Peter Doherty founded The Libertines and is now frontman of Babyshambles

Chris Donald is a chubby, balding ex-*Viz* editor, author, pile sufferer and bad tempered father-of-three

Richard Donkin is the author of *Blood, Sweat and Tears, the Evolution of Work (Texere)*

Chris Draper is an illustrator and beekeeper who regularly contributes to *New Scientist* and the *Independent*

Bill Drummond is a serial father

Hannah Dyson draws anthropomorphic creatures and other beings

David Hallows is an illustrator discovering the beauty of old Stax recordings

Paul Hamilton regrets nothing, not the divorce, the bankruptcy, the homelessness or the prison record. He would do it all again, except sit through *Love Actually*

Jeff Harrison is a painter, illustrator and misanthropist from east London

Joe Harrison is a comical, talented all-round good guy, need we say more?

Clare Hatcher is a very talented lady

Anthony Haythornthwaite is an illustrator for hire, to contact him email anthony@aqhthestudio.co.uk

Will Hodgkinson is a journalist based in London and is writing a book about the guitar

Will Hogan is a raconteur, scribe and used ad salesman. He's available at will@idler.co.uk

Aaron Howdle is a designer and illustrator who loves robots. His work can be seen at www.aaronhowdle.co.uk

Sandra Howgate has been busy illustrating for various publications, and not had enough time for idle pleasures

Tony Husband is an award winning cartoonist who works for the *Times*, the *Express*, the *Sun*, *Private Eye* and many many more. He also performs a live cartoon poetry interactive stage show with Ian Macmillan. For more information visit tonyhusband.co.uk

Alex James lives in a very big house in the country

Fanny Johnstone writes about sex and cars in the *Daily Telegraph*

Pat Kane is a musician and writes on the ethics of play. He is author of *The Play Ethic* (Macmillan). www.theplayethic .com

Andrew Kendall is a rock'n'roll photo-grapher and multi-media man

Dan Kieran is an amateur philosopher who wants to know if you're happy. Email dan@idler.co.uk

Chloe King is an illustrator. She can be found at rideem@boozers.moonfruit.com

Rowley Leigh is head chef at Kensington Place, food writer for the *FT* and author of *No Place Like Home*

PAT KANE

SONIA ORTIZ ALCÓN

ALEX JAMES

SOPHIE LODGE

Rafaella Malaguti is an Italian journalist who works on *Il Manifesto*

Yahia Lababidi is an Egyptian/Lebanese poet currently working as editor for UNESCO's Cairo office

Sophie Lodge is an illustrator and on her way back to New Zealand to work on King-Kong

Pete Loveday is a jobbing artist, self-buried in Devon. He created the legendary Russell comics. Find out more at ccnewz.com

Edwin Marney is an illustrator who generally works for dull business magazines. Visit his website at edwinmarney.co.uk

Marcus Oakley is still learning to play the guitar

Sonia Ortiz Alcón laid out this mag and her work can be seen at foreignoffice.com

Kevin Parr is a writer and angler. He can sometimes be found on the A33 near Winchester

Joe Piercy teaches, writes and raises kids in Brighton

Clare Pollard is an international poet and dramatist

John Riordan thinks Western culture peaked with Motown. He really, really wants a cat

Greg Rowland is a legitimate businessman

Nick Roberts

Edward Sage is the *Idler*'s Managing Editor

Linda Scott is an illustrator and her email address is lindapix7@yahoo.co.uk

Paul Slade is a freelance journalist

Jack Thurston is a former Labour Party advisor

Gwyn Vaughn Roberts lives in Wales and can only produce work when his mental state is a fine balance of energy and `misery

Vince is an illustrator and here is his website.

Ian Vince is a left-handed, Mac-compatible, asthmatic comedy writer, clearly looking for some kind of niche market. He runs socialscrutiny.org

Walshworks illustrations can be found at www.eastwing.co.uk and www.walshworks. org.uk

Chris Watson has a new t-shirt label at www.tonuppress.com and his work can be seen at www.chris-watson.co.uk

Tony White is the *Idler*'s Literary Editor. He's just co-edited (with Matt Thorne and Borivoj Radakovic) a new fiction anthology called Croation Nights, which is published by Serpent's Tail

Chris Yates is a legendary fisherman, photographer, master of idleness and author of *The Secret Carp* (Merlin Unwin)

NOTES
FROM
THE
COUCH

JEFF HARRISON

THE IDLER'S DIARY

THE GUARDIAN reports that thirtysomethings are turning off work in their droves. A study commissioned by Employers' Forum on Age, a body campaigning on age issues in the workplace, reported that only 54% of thirtysomethings actually enjoy working. The study concludes: "People of all ages are motivated to change and develop, but are being held back by an outdated idea of careers where young people start at the bottom and retirement is a cliff edge at the peak." Well, we could have told you that. Us idlers, it seems, are ahead of the game. The answer: quite your job! Or as the situationists put it, "Ne Travaillez Jamais".

THIS IS THE first issue that we are publishing with Ebury, the esteemed enormo-publishers. This will mean that for the first time the Idler will be widely available in bookshops and that maybe, just maybe, after twelve years more or less underground, we are starting to get mainstream appeal.

WE WELCOME the appointment of Ruth Kelly as Secretary of State for education. It's good to have a Catholic in the cabinet as it is currently dominated by members of the Protestant pro-work, anti-pleasure tradition. Perhaps Ruth might introduce a few radical concepts into schools, things like fun, creativity and hope rather than obsessing with academic tests and simply preparing people for a so-called competitive job market.

WE ARE PLEASED to announce two more births to Idler staff: to Dan Kieran a son called Wilfred, and to Tom Hodgkinson a son called Henry.

IN THE 1930S, Himmler sent out a directive called Operation Workshy. He asked that all Labour Exchanges pass the names of all those fit to work but who refused work to the SS. The SS then rounded up the idlers and sent them to work camps, where they had a black triangle sewn on to their uniform. The idea was that they should learn the value of hard work. We might wonder whether little has changed, when we see in the papers the

latest New Labour initiative to get us back to work. Blair's latest attack has been on the disabled.

A LICENCE TO SKIVE

NOW HERE'S SOMETHING that might interest you: on the weekend of June 17-19, we are putting on an idling course. Camp Idle will take place at Dial House, the arts centre created by CRASS founder Penny Rimbaud. Your tutors for the weekend will be Tom Hodgkinson, John Nicholson and Penny Rimbaud. There will be fine food and fine talking and we hope to put on a weekend that will be fun as well as useful to those pursuing the idle life. Email Tom on tom@idler.co.uk for more details.

THE PAPERBACK of Idler editor Tom Hodgkinson's book *How To Be Idle* is out in the summer, and to celebrate we are declaring 1 July to be an unofficial bank holiday. Saint Simeon's Day is named after a crazy medieval saint who hung out with ne'er do wells and liked going about naked, and we urge all readers to phone in sick or just exercise your liberty to take a day off. We don't have enough bank holidays in Britain and it's time to do something about it.

LONDON TRANSPORT bosses came to the aid of the cities workers in February when they encouraged people to skip work before a flake of snow had even fallen. Business leaders bleated about a "skivers charter" the following day when the expected snow then failed to materialise. London's workers, meanwhile, kicked of their shoes and enjoyed an unexpected day off. 🌀

READERS' LETTERS

Write to us at: **The Idler**, Studio 20, 24-28A Hatton Wall, London EC1N 8JH or tom@idler.co.uk

EVERY LETTER WINS AN IDLER MUG!

AM I IDLE? Oh yes, very much so. Not only am I a civil servant, where idleness is as inherent as addiction to sarcasm and tea, but I am also a mental mountaineer, which requires me to only think about climbing the great peaks of the world without pain and tiredness.

I am not in work at the moment, having taken a day off to look after my son who is asleep conveniently, and am simply looking out of the window at my shed. Is this not what days off are for? Have recently read Tom's book and enjoyed it thoroughly.
Paul McGrath

I WAS DOING a Google search for "Getting to bed on time", and went to your web site to the article "Getting out of bed on time". If I could go to bed when I should, I don't think I'd have a problem with getting up, but for a number of reasons, I have an extremely difficult time getting my butt into bed at a reasonable hour. I end up staying up the entire night doing piddley kinds of things, and finally conking out about 5am, and I'm worthless for the day. This happens night after night, month after month. It's ruining my life! I'm trying to keep a home business afloat, but it's mired in the mud.

Any ideas? I'm forty-nine, currently divorced and living alone, and have my two sons over two or three nights a week.
Will in San Diego, California Drink beer.

BEING ISOLATED down here in the Antipodes, I have only just discovered your fine publication. I am ecstatic with the reflection of my personal philosophy, which I have striven to have recognised by the system which I have the misfortune to "work" in. I am viewed by many within it as an inveterate idler, a term used in the perjorative. They however find it difficult to do without me as I am developing significant skills in being knowledgeable in certain key areas. Along with the concept of being an idler, I have been long known as a cynic; a grossly abused term given the fine traditions of Antisthenes and Diogenes. The people who most often accuse me of this tend to be those who are the most cynical themselves in their enslavery to productivity and financial outcomes. Anyway, enough of the ravings, I just had to let you know of my existence in Aoteroa/New Zealand.
ka Kite Ano (That's PC talk for see you later)
Murray Edgar

I AM WRITING with regards to "How to be a Pop Star" by Eddie Argos and Keith Mahoney (Winter 2004).
In it, they said "Epileptic Firing Squad - the less said about them, the better". I am the guitarist in the aforementioned band, and I'd like to make it clear that we are fucking amazing. I love Eddie and Keith to bits but they are a pair of cheeky bastards for saying that, and I was upset for at least three minutes.

In the forthcoming issue, would you be so kind as to redress this error by writing something to say that we are brilliant? With songs like "Anne Franks' Drumkit" how can we be crap?
Matthew Hockridge

I HAVE ONLY just learned of your mag; so, in case you don't know, here are three sources on the virtues of doing nothing: the original would be the *Rubiyat of Omar Kyham*, but not the Edward Fitzgerald version. This work from 12th century Persia. Book by Lin Yutang *The Importance of Living*, published 1930, is probably the best there is. *The Way of Chuang Tzu* by Thomas Merton has many samples, as in: "The active life – what a pity"! I've been of the lazy mind for over thirty years, so I assure you these three are the best.
VM

I LIKE MEETING other people as lazy as me but generally can't be bothered to stay in touch. I've tried seeking help. I found a support group for the terminally lethargic but not only could I not be bothered to attend, when I called up they couldn't be bothered to return my call and I've subsequently discovered that none of the ten million registered members can be arsed to turn up either. In the light of the fact that laziness has recently overtaken fishing as this country's largest participation sport, (although personally I didn't get around replying to the census form I recieved for some reason). Anyway the point I am making is... oh who cares?
Tom Radford

I DISCOVERED THE book *How To Be Idle* in a bookstore in a foreign town and collapsed on to the nearest mini-stool to read it. I have no idea how long I spent reading it but I read most of it chuckling loudly. That book genuinely allows me to feel less guilty for cultivating my idle streak. I am now 33 years of age. Up until I was 28, I worked like a demon. My labour was manual with the resultant whippet-like physique and giddy mind. A work accident (broken arm), gave me my first introduction to the sedentary life. Oh, happy days! I look back on those days as epiphanies, the dozes in front of MTV, the cats and dogs that I hung out with at the time, the sheer healing power of those no-brainer days (daze), all wrapped in a gloriously hot summer. I never went back to the life of manual work. I got a job in a small office. This arrangement allows me to come to work long after the rush hour has passed and I'm home whenever I want to really. I'm thriving on my lifestyle. My girlfriend reckons I purr in the morning. I catnap every day. I'm writing this as a nod to all my idler brothers and sisters. How delicious are our lives? Hear! hear! to the joys of being idle, I feel that I'm going to live forever!
Michael Hanley

I ABSOLUTELY LOVE your site! Just stumbled across it in the course of killing my 12 or 14 hours a day on the internet. I myself am a professional ne'r-do-well. Being a ne'r-do-well is not

READERS' LETTERS

for everybody. It's a nasty job, but someone has to take it on. After all, what would the rest of you do if you didn't have the local ne'r-do-well to compare your own life against? How many of you have not at some time thought or even said, "Well, I may be a Republican (writer, accountant, axe-murderer, etc.), but at least I'm not as bad as so-and-so? Generally, ne'r-do-wells are born and not made. Given the nature of the profession, many of those who take up the occupation find their calling later in life than most. It is only after failure after failure – dropping out of numerous educational programs, being fired from many jobs, getting rejection letters from vanity presses, having a long list of ex-lovers and failed marriages, former friends who have hired hit men against you, that the light finally begins to dawn.

In my own case, I was a mere child of forty and had moved back in with Mom for the 10th or 12th time when my path finally became clear. I was laying on my bed, eating a large sack of pork rinds and watching "Leave it to Beaver" re-runs when Mom poked her head into my room, stared with distaste at my over flowing ash tray of half smoked Winston cigarettes, my broken dreams scattered here and there in untidy stacks, and my own dis-shelved state and announced, "See? What did I always tell you? You'll never amount to a damn thing! I should have listened to your father and had the abortion while I still could!" With that pronouncement, she then turned and slammed shut my door, and I could hear her outraged mutterings as she harrumphed down to the kitchen to pour herself a stiff drink. It was a moment of pure Satori. I'd found my place in life at last! The wide world of ne'r-do-well-dom opened its doors and beckoned alluringly to me. No one else wanted me, so I jumped at the chance.

I began to hang out in places like coffee shops and bars and public libraries. I wrote volumes of poetry so bad that even homeless people refused to used the paper on which it was written to start camp fires. I joined both the Communist and the anarchist parties. My Mom kicked me out onto the streets for the last time and refused to recognize me when we chanced to meet down at the thrift shop. I attended professional meetings of ne'r-do-wells where I was the only one in attendance – everyone else didn't have the gas money to drive two miles to get there or were too busy messing up their lives to take time off to attend. I leapt into this leadership vacuum at once and got drunk. Ten years later I remembered I was a member of a professional organization of which I was president and sent myself an IOU for my dues.

I became a champion of lost causes and involved myself in activities such as the search for intelligent life on US army bases and the attempt to chew gum and scratch my nose at the same time.

I am pleased to find a group of like-minded souls at The Idler. Keep up the good work (or not)!
Marichiko

I FELT I should write after seeing the latest edition in which you ask, "have you succeeded in becoming an idler?" Well, I think I have and it's partly down to your fine publication. The *Idler* struck a chord with me in about 1998. I was on the dole at the time and there was a piece in one edition by someone who always dreaded people asking him what he did. I knew how he felt. There was a lot of other good stuff as well so I decided to subscribe, but you promptly went bust. Someone sent me a couple of back issues as a consolation though.

Anyway, by the time I saw the magazine had reappeared as some kind of periodical I was working at the *Yorkshire Post* in Leeds. On paper it was a good job with good money as well, but it left me empty and worn out, longing for the time to do stuff I really wanted to do. This didn't make sense, I'd played the career game, done quite well but it just left me feeling shit. And this is the feeling that you and your colleagues have articulated so well. I found it immensely reassuring to know other people had the same outlook and it was one of your editorials, which talked about not living life in the service of the future or something, that helped give me the confidence to resign. That was nearly a year ago and I'm still alive, I can still afford food and clothes. The world didn't end. I now do freelance journalism part-time and I'm a film student the other time, so sometimes I'm probably too busy, but I'm using my time to do what I want. And that's a big breakthrough. So, thanks very much.

Anon 🐌

I D L E R E D I T I O N S

SKIVERS

HEROES AND VILLAINS...

JEANETTE WINTERSON

THE GREEN MAN, DEVON

Jeanette Winterson

The author of *Oranges Are Not The Only Fruit* has turned the downstairs of her Spitalfields home into a delicatessen and grocers. "Oranges are not our only fruit (we also have bananas five for a pound and a lovely bunch of organic coconuts." Truly she is sexing the glace cherry.

Back Burner

We are always having our ideas put on the back burner, which is a nice place to be as it saves us the work of putting them into practice. Perhaps one day we will move from the Hob Of Creativity to gently brown under the Ideas Grill.

Red Button on Your Remote

Stop trying to make us press it, you buggers. Tear up that interactive revenue business plan now. The only red button we want on our TV is one that instantly pornolizes whatever we are watching, from *Rosemary And Thyme* to *Animal Hospital*.

The Parsnip

This amazingly slow-growing vegetable takes eight to ten months to turn from seed into an edible specimen, but my, it's worth the wait. For such gigantic, tapering beasts to grow from a tiny flake-like seed is a miracle in itself, but they are also among the sweetest of vegetables and, what's more, can be used to make a delicious wine. Ignore them at your peril.

The Pub

Because I'm Worth It.

Piers Morgan

The exuberant and spirited former *Daily Mirror* editor has effectively retired while still under forty, living on redundancy and book royalties, the dream of every Idler. From working all hours and living in state of constant stress he is now free at last, to write books and maybe do a little light presenting work. We applaud his playful nature and welcome him to the brotherhood of freelance wanderers.

STRIVERS

...OF THE IDLE UNIVERSE

JIMMY CARR

HAROLD PINTER

Jimmy Carr

Presenter of the endless *100 Cheapest Clips* shows, Channel 4 are intent in riding Jimmy into the ground before putting him out to pasture at the BBC, much like their previous exhausted nags, Graham Norton and Dom Joly. As if the spirit of Bob Monkhouse became trapped in a waxwork dummy.

Crazy Frog Ringtone

This year's Billy Bass singing fish, its popularity makes you despair of your fellow citizens, that hopeless shower of shit. While the rest of us log our guts out, the demons behind Crazy Frog sodomise one another with rolled sheaves of banknotes and cackle.

Automated Excuse Lady

As heard apologizing in railway stations across the land. When the robots rise up and take their rightful place as our masters, they will force mankind to stand trial for this torment. The lady computer on the North London Line says sorry forty times an hour – and it's not even her fault.

Harold Pinter

Before America escalates the conflict with Iran. It should consider the dire consequences – another anti-war poem from Harold Pinter.

Culture Show

BBC2's bourgeoisathon designed to ensure charter renewal. Mariella Frostrup, Andrew Marr and the gang spout empty promises in the on-going drive to force otherwise decent people to take a greater interest in "the arts", for the sole purpose of furthering the careerist, status ambitions of BBC wonks. Do you like the "arts"? Do you support the "arts"? Or does the very mention of "the arts" make your arse fall off in despair?

The Runs

What's all the hurry, my shit? From now on, constipation shall be known as an attack of "the crawls".

Wanadoo

Like a rakish lover, these guys will do anything for your credit card details and then they'll drop you, abandon you. Broadband my arse. For twenty pounds a month you could send 76 letters first class.

TONY HUSBAND'S JOKE PAGE

KNOWN TO HIS FRIENDS AS THE WORLD'S WORST JOKE TELLER, TONY HUSBAND ASKS A FEW FAMOUS FACES FOR THEIR FAVOURITE GAGS.

Terry Jones

A truck driver is delivering some penguins to a zoo in a refrigerated truck. The truck breaks down and the penguins start to over-heat so he flags down another refrigerated truck.
Driver: "If I give you fifty quid will you take these penguins to the zoo?"
2nd Driver: "Sure, load them in the back."
They do and he drives off. Hours later his truck has been repaired and he's driving through the town and he sees the second driver leading the penguins down a street, he pulls over.
Driver: "What are you doing?"
2nd Driver: "Well, I took them to the zoo and I've got some change from the fifty quid so I'm taking them to the pictures."

Phil Pope

Q: How many surrealists does it take to change a lightbulb?
A: Fish

Guy Garvey – (From Elbow)

Q: What did the cow say to the farmer?
A: "Why do you never kiss me when you're playing with my tits?"

Michael Palin

Have you heard the one about the insomniac, the agnostic and the dyslexic who stayed awake all night wondering if there was a dog?

Tim Aitkin – (Wine Expert)

A blind man was given a cheesegrater. He said it was the most violent book he'd ever read.

Ian McMillan

A man walks into a library and says "Can I have a pint of bitter please?"
The librarian replies, "This is a library."
The man, in a whispered tone, says, "Sorry, can I have a pint of bitter please?"

Mel Smith

A man goes to the psychiatrist and says, "I think I'm a dog."
The psychiatrist says, "Well, lie on the couch."
And the man replies "I'm not allowed on the couch."

Tony Husband

A man goes to see his grandad and finds him sat engrossed at the kitchen table.
Man: "What are you doing, grandad?"
Grandad: "Trying to do this jigsaw of this fuckin' hen."
Man: "Grandad, put the cornflakes back in the box and get to bed."

THE FINE LINE BETWEEN

MICE **MEN**

MICE	MEN
Like to breed at night	But not really fussy either way
Like to run up women's skirts	Like to run their hands up women's skirts
Exhibit prominent scrotum	Will attempt this when drunk
Can squeeze through a hole the size of a pencil	Will also attempt this when drunk
Humane traps	Marriage
Inhumane traps	Marriage, then divorce
Will eat any old leftover food	"Are you going to finish that?"
Make women jump on chairs	Make women jump through hoops
Hard to catch	Commitment issues
They ran after the farmer's wife	Because she was easy
Vermin	Scum

NICK ROBERTS

FREE AT LAST

Water closet philosopher Chris Donald on the many pleasures
of retreating to the loo. Illustrations by Hannah Dyson

I read a lot of books in the toilet. Apart from trains and planes, the toilet's the only place I can read books. I've just finished Bob Dylan's *Chronicles Volume One*, which took me about 28 stools from cover to cover. With respect to Bob Dylan, it's not the sort of book you'd read anywhere else. I even read Jeremy Paxman's dreary book *The English* from cover to cover while sitting on the lavatory.

In the past I've bought armchairs specifically to sit and read in. I've positioned them carefully alongside bookcases and adjacent to warm coal fires. Then I've sat in them and picked up a book, but it never seems to work. Given the choice between reading a book and gazing at the coal fire, I'll always go for the fire. If there is no fire I'll gaze happily at the carpet, or the skirting boards, or the curtains. I'm far too easily distracted by everyday things to read a book in a comfortable chair. And when you have a wife and three kids and a dog in the house, you're far too exposed sitting in a chair out in the open. If you're in an armchair and children start fighting, you get up and intervene. If you're in an armchair and the phone rings,

you feel obliged to answer it. But it's different when you're on the toilet, with your trousers round your ankles. Only in that sacred position do you find sanctuary from the bedlam of domestic life.

Toilets are very personal places. I'm extremely reluctant to use someone else's toilet. Use it properly, that is. My aunty has a toilet I could never sit on. There's something about the twee decor, the yellow lavatory seat and seat cover, the matching loo roll, the pine framed mirror on the door, the toothbrushes on the window sill, the fluffy carpet. It's like a dolls' house toilet, never intended to be used. I'm sure she uses it – logic tells me she must – but I have a problem even peeing in it. I'd be far more comfortable shitting on her back lawn right outside the French windows than I would in that pristine little chapel at the top of her stairs.

I've recently been tracing my dad's family tree, and I've discovered that when my dad was growing up in Newcastle in the 1930s his family had to share a single outside lavatory with seven other households. Life must have been unbearable. Things have come full circle since then. My family now have seven toilets to choose from scattered around our rambling country house. We have the cloakroom WC under the stairs, an upstairs WC at the top of the stairs, a bathroom with WC, a small WC opposite, a downstairs bathroom with WC, a garage WC and of course the gardener's WC. But I only read books in the cloakroom WC, which is very much my own private place.

It's a narrow little room with a high ceiling, dark green carpet and wood panelled walls. There's a nice warm radiator right alongside the

lavatory, and on the floor beneath the small window there's a magazine rack stuffed with old railway magazines. I look at the railway magazines when I'm between books. Above the magazine rack is the window sill where I keep my pile ointment and my books. The pile ointment is there for two reasons. There's the obvious one of course, which my wife says is down to bad posture (I say it was because I pushed too hard as a child, but I shan't go into that now.) But that greasy little tube is also there to ward off intruders, to make them feel uncomfortable. My wife goes to great lengths to try and entice strangers into my toilet and make it a pleasant place for them to linger. She hides my pile ointment behind the mirror on the window sill, and she sprays air freshener and perfume about the place. She threw out my old railway magazines the other day and replaced them with copies of *House Beautiful*, no doubt to remind guests that our house is beautiful, more so than theirs. And with nicer smelling toilets too.

My wife doesn't like me going to the toilet, reading my books and wallowing in my own perfectly natural perfumes. She can't reasonably deny me my visits to the loo but she'll impose herself on proceedings by asking where I'm going every time I head towards the cloakroom. Or she'll stand outside the door and ask "Are you in there?" when she knows perfectly well I am. Or she'll make me a cup of tea and shout to tell me that it's going cold.

We all need our own space, and in a house as big as ours one small water closet is not an unreasonable amount of space to ask for. If an Englishman's home is his castle, then my castle walls fell many years ago under siege from the outside world. But that lavatory is my keep. And it is there beneath the stairs that I shall make my stand – or I shall sit defiantly at any rate – reading whatever books and magazines I like. For as long as I like. ◑

DO NOT USE INSTRUCTIONS

Here's how to use those tricky boxer shorts and nodding dog

THE BOXER SHORT

Instructions for use:
Hold the boxer short up. Is it clean? Then proceed.

1. Hook a thumb in opposite sides of the elasticated waistband to open up the layout of the short. You should be able to discern three crucial holes. The small flap-like aperture represents the front of the shorts while the other two parallel holes are for your legs.

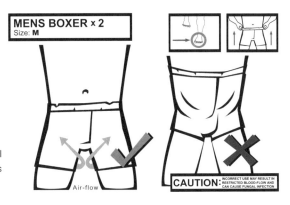

MENS BOXER x 2
Size: **M**

Air-flow

CAUTION: INCORRECT USE MAY RESULT IN RESTRICTED BLOOD-FLOW AND CAN CAUSE FUNGAL INFECTION

2. From a secure, sitting position, carefully insert one leg – foot first – into its corresponding hole. Do not attempt to insert both legs simultaneously. Now lower your other leg – also foot first – into the remaining hole and slowly raise the elasticated waistband until the short covers your loins.

3. Be careful not to overshoot the raising of the short. When you feel a tight pressure pain around the scrotum, you should cease the upward pulling motion upon the waistband.
Congratulations. Now you are ready to start enjoying the benefits of the boxer short.

4. The aperture at the front of the shorts is to effect the speedy removal of the penis in case of urination. Please take care to shake the penis vigorously before attempting to return it to the shorts as stray drops of urine may fall upon the short.

5. After twelve hours of use, please remove the boxer short and discard it into the corner of the room.

6. The manufacturer is not responsible for injuries incurred by the misuse of this boxer short.

NODDING DOG

Instructions for use: Congratulations on purchasing the Roncon Rover Nodding Dog. Remove from box. Tap head gently with the red index finger to commence nodding. Position the Roncon Rover Nodding Dog in a warm, quiet environment with plenty of comic effect.
The nodding of this dog does not necessarily represent the opinion of the manufacturer unless specifically stated. This nodding is intended solely for the use of the individual or entity to which it is addressed. The nodding of this dog is not to be taken as trustworthy counsel. If a question is addressed to the nodding dog, and it nods, this reply does not necessarily represent the manufacturer encouraging the purchaser to undertake a course of action, such as murder. 🌀

AARON HOWDLE

MDA

THE KEN KORDA COLUMN

Ken talks to Adam Buxton about his fave things

I've always had a passion for facts. Can't help it. I consume facts as if they were Chilli flavoured Walkers Sensations. As a result my friends (who include many of the cast of the *The Office*) are often putting questions to me about this, that or 'tother and I thought it might be a nice idea to compile some of the most delicious for publication in a small pamphlet style book which could be sold next to the amusing parodies of the *Little Book of Calm* that you find in Tower records and the such. Sadly no bastard wants to help me out so until the fuckwits who run these so called publishing companies come to their senses, here's a little tastette of what they're missing. If you have any similar enquiries don't hesitate to write in and I'll get back to you.

The UK has the Beatles as the best rock/pop band of all time. Who are the American equivalent?

This is a tricky one because "best" is such a subjective term. Are we talking about "best" in terms of record sales, song craft, fashion savvy or simply the "best" overall? If indeed we are talking about the best overall American band of all time, I think most people would agree that it is Hootie & The Blowfish. Or The Georgia Satellites. Now let that be an end to it.

How do French people remember which nouns are masculine and which feminine?

There are a couple of answers to this one. Some French people do what we would do and simply carry a small dictionary. However the most common method of remembering is known as "remembering words", which is kind of a French version of the way we in England remember words.

Basically you learn to speak a language and then it kind of stays in your brain.

Where does the phrase "I don't give a monkey's" come from, meaning: "I don't care"?

A monkey's what? I'm afraid the answer is a little fruity, but it's "nuts". You see monkeys are famously fond of

nuts (as in peanuts) and to give a monkey's nuts away would drive them indigo. Hence "I don't give a monkey's" meaning "I'm not the kind of person who would steal from a monkey". Also it might have something to do with testes.

When will I, will be famous?

I can't answer, I can't answer that.

On The Bill and similar, why are prostitutes referred to as 'Toms'. I guess it is rhyming slang but what?

I've heard many an answer to this particular query and they're all quite well meant but I'm sorry to say, entirely wrong. Referring to profit-sluts or "Charlottes" as "Toms" originates from the classic song "Space Oddity" by David Bowie. The song's protagonist Major Tom is left "sitting in a tin can, far from the world" very much like...a prostitute! *Ecce Romani.*

What's another word for synonym?

Another word could be "sametimename" but it's not widely used. Except by me.

What is the origin of the expression "Utmost fish"?

I think you'll find "Utmost fish" is not a real expression. (I am indebted for the above to Bostock Harrisole's book *Is Utmost Fish An Expression Or Not?*)

Is it correct to say "The audience are applauding" or "The audience is applauding"?

The Hollywood screenwriter JRR Tolkien was asked this very question by *Grease 2* star, Michelle Pfeiffer. Tolkien thought for eight days then replied "Michelle, you may say whichever you pfeiffer" Michelle wasn't amused and was reported to have called Tolkein "a filthy faggot with a dirty freak's brain." In fact the answer she was looking for is "the audiences aren't applauding."

How much would an English one pound note with Isaac Newton on it be worth today?

That note is no longer legal tender and as such it's worth nothing at all. However, supposing it were indeed still a valid item of currency I'd hazard a guess at it being worth around one pound.

When will Jimmy Carr run out?

This is a very popular question with a surprising

> Michelle wasn't amused and was reported to have called Tolkein "a filthy faggot with a dirty freak's brain"

answer. Amazingly Jimmy Carr will never run out because the one liner maestro and Channel 4 boss has accumulated a body of work so vast it has been placed in a giant shaft that leads directly to the earth's core where it feeds the planet with chuckles. Those chuckles then filter back up through the inner core, the outer core, and the lower mantle where they mix with giggles and nebulous desperation. They then proceed the rest of the way through the upper mantle and the transition region, emerging from the earth's crust as commissions for new light entertainment formats. It was once thought that Tony Slattery might be a similarly inexhaustible source of yoks, but sadly the depletion of the Ho Ho Hozone layer through over-use during the late eighties destroyed him.

Why aren't the letters on a computer keyboard in alphabetical order?

They just aren't.
OK I'm fed up with this now. I'm going now bye! Ken. ☻

CHINESE VEGAN

Iain Aitch on London's mysterious meat free eateries.
Illustration by Foreign Office

Being something of a full time flâneur definitely has its advantages. Sure, the remuneration may not be as attractive or as regular as something which comes with a pay scale, career ladder and regular "evaluation" from someone wearing a novelty tie, but it does afford you the luxury of lunching at your leisure. So instead of joining the masses rushing back to the office with a semi-frozen triangle of something mushy between polystyrene-like bread I get to saunter, select and sit down.

Milling around the back streets of Soho or Bloomsbury at around 1.45pm is the finest time to select a lunch venue. Not only does this mean that you will have your selection of the rapidly emptying tables, but it also means that you can take your seat content in the knowledge that everyone else around you is about to head off back to an afternoon of office tedium. Nothing makes a man so content in his idleness as the thought of others about to work.

On one of my perambulations a couple of years ago I came across Tai, which is a vegan buffet restaurant in Soho's

Greek Street that serves a mixture of Chinese and Thai-style food. Much of the food involves fake meat products made from gluten or soya, such as soya "chicken" in black bean sauce, or sweet and sour "chicken". Harking back (albeit somewhat soya-ham fistedly) to the vegetarian cuisine of the court of an ancient Buddhist emperor and making the assumption that most animals taste like chicken anyhow, Tai straddled the line between healthy and greasy with aplomb. It didn't look that appetising, in fact a friend and I dubbed it "dog food" after its choice-chunks appearance, but it certainly tasted good.

On a walk toward Trafalgar Square one day I noticed what appeared to be another branch of Tai. This one was called Chi and looked almost identical. Situated on St Martin's Lane, it had the same £5 "all you can eat" deal as well as the same red fascia and cheap tables. I went in and ate, finding the selection of pretend dead things near identical too.

Before long it seemed that Tai clones were popping up all over central London, all of them with similar décor and food; all of them offering you the opportunity to gorge on soya pork, beef or chicken for a fiver. This rapid franchising seemed somewhat odd to me, but who was I to question it, after all I now had a choice of five vegan buffets, from Euston Road in the north to St Martin's Lane to the south, as well as an ever-growing number on the outskirts of town. For some reason I was most regularly drawn to Joi on Percy Street, which sits at the centre of the five and it was whilst wondering why this was that revelation hit. Above me was Wai on Goodge Street and then CTJ on Euston Road. Below me was Tai on Greek Street and Chi on St Martin's Lane. I drew a mental line in my head. All of these restaurants were situated along a straight line.

After stuffing myself with more prawnless prawn toast and paying my £5 I set out towards Chi, imagining that I was travelling as the crow flies and painting a line as I went. I stopped at the Waterstones near the corner of Oxford Street to sneak a look in an A–Z. It seemed that my theory was correct. And what is more the line cut right through St Martin's-in-the Field.

Having a rudimentary knowledge of the psychogeography of the capital I was aware that the church on this site is the starting point on a major ley line that runs along the Strand. This had a whole range of theories flashing through my mind. Was it part of some vast vegan conspiracy to harness the power of the ley? Was it restaurant *feng shui* on a giant scale? Or was it just a coincidence?

After studying the evidence I am hoping that coincidence is the answer. After all, the line of CTJ, Wai, Joi, Tai and Chi joins the Strand at the exact point of the Subway sandwich bar opposite Charing Cross station and another branch of the malodorous chain sits on the line where it hits Oxford Street. If the line is being used to exploit psychic power then the energy is being filtered through grilled, rubbery cheese and nothing good (nor vegan for that matter) can come of that.

In the meantime my research continues at Joi. I can recommend the red curry with "beef", or indeed any other of the dishes that require inverted commas. 🐚

Joi is at 14 Percy Street, London W1. CTJ, Wai, Tai and Chi can be found along the axis between Euston Road and St Martin's-in-the-Field.

SPACE MAN

Alex James on the eternal fillability of the endless shed

The first thing about sheds is that they fill up. Suitcases do that too. They just get full, now matter how big they are. You can't have an empty shed for very long, they have a gravitational field so powerful that nothing, not even shite, can escape. I know this because I live on a farm. A farm is a combination of fields and sheds. When I came into my sheds, I didn't know what was going to go in there. There were some sheep living in one of them, which worked nicely, but the big barn has become a kind of personal Victoria and Albert museum. Instead of throwing stuff away I put it in the shed. It started with the old B.M.W, then an old kitchen got stored there, logs followed, aggregates, roof tiles. Bricks; and that's just the big hangar. There's a small room as well, and that's where old paperwork accumulates. Everything. All the boring stuff that you have to deal with is in the office, but once it's in the shed it's just scenery. Because it's in the past, nothing in the sheds is ever heavy or scary.

It's a bit like flying, sitting there with the paper rail of your life at arm's length. I'm pretty sure it'll all come in handy, maybe it won't, but it's quite nice just having it all there.

There is a real sense of peace in a proper shed, of stillness. By the time

DAVID HALLOWS

SHED HEAVEN

anything gets to the shed it's had all the marketing and frills rubbed off, which makes a shed and a garage different. A garage is for stuff that you're using that has a specific role. It has to be kept tidy. It is impossible to have a perfectly tidy shed, as this would require an infinite amount of time. Sheds always need tidying, but the person who the shed belongs to can always find what they are looking for immediately. It is not clear whether tidying a shed ever makes it any tidier. Stuff is just its existential essence in there. An old car is just the sum of its parts. It's one step away from the dustbin, which is how we should treat all the merchandise in our lives. You can't get creative with stuff unless you can feel bigger than it. It's hard to feel bigger than something with a really strong brand identity, say like a new BMW.

It is vital to feel like the king of the castle, as somehow or other bigger than your car. It's getting harder, though. It's the way it's all going, we're all starting to become dwarfed and swamped by the identity of our possessions. All the stuff we have to deal with has Godlike qualities. It's like living in ancient Greece. There are so many gods around. Marketing takes a pair of shoes and turns them into something mythical. It's a lazy way to get noticed, having a flash pair of trainers. Get them in the shed and kick ass. 🐌

AN ACTOR'S LIFE FOR ME

Want a career where you're not even working when
you're at work? Try acting. By Reuben Morgan

Actors have long got away with the lie that their job is the hardest job in the world. If the greatest trick the Devil played is convincing the world he didn't exist, then the lie that the actor's job is hard is the trick the Devil wants to know how to do. I love it when I read interviews where actors go on about their "work", their "craft" and their "business". I love it, then I scoff. For actors are all simply kids who are allowed to play with the dressing up box day after day while the rest of the population does something worthwhile.

For example, a day acting in a film involves large periods of sitting around waiting for the people who do the real work on a movie set such as electricians, set decorators, camera operators and make-up artists to do their thing.

Then the actor comes on, does a little bit of actual acting which involves saying words someone else has already gone to the bother of thinking up and typing, and standing in places a director has already worked out, while wearing clothes and holding things someone else has chosen

for them. And then they sit back down again in trailers or dressing rooms or in chairs that have their names on.

And if that seems like it might be hard work, the truth is that scenes involving more than one actor, a director usually films at least twice. Once with a camera on actor one doing his lines and reactions to the other person's lines, and then again with the camera facing actor two. While actor two is being filmed, actor one does his lines with none of the gusto and professionalism he was putting into them when the camera was on him since, you know, what's the point? Even less work than at first glance, then.

Stage actors also have it easy. Unless you are playing a part where the play you are in is named after you such as *Hamlet* or *Mary Poppins*, you are likely to spend most of your time off stage waiting to come on and act. And even when you are on stage and presumably acting, the likelihood is you aren't speaking most of the time. You might be listening to what another character has to say about the fact that they are mad north by northwest or what exactly it is that helps the medicine go down. That again is not real acting, no matter what an actor will say. It's listening. It involves no further effort than ensuring you have a working set of ears.

And for the rest of the day while you're not speaking, or listening, you sit around at home waiting for the show. You might look out of the window in the morning, but the danger of doing so is you may find you then have nothing to do in the afternoon.

But am I ignoring the work that goes on before

the show goes on? A play must be rehearsed before it is put on and this involves the real hard work. Well. . .

Rehearsals are notoriously long days where nothing much gets achieved over and over again. You meet in a Church hall far too early – Jiminy Cricket's observation of an actor's rising time is perfectly accurate, but during rehearsals an 11am start is just about manageable – in some awful street somewhere south of the Thames. You drink bad coffee, smoke cigarettes and walk around without even knowing the words you're going to say. You watch how everyone else is doing their parts then you slyly nick their best tricks for your performance. Then it's down to the pub for a moan about the director, theatrical agents, other actors in the play and ones they have worked with before and etcetera etcetera.

So that's an actor's working life covered. But of course most of the time 100% of the acting profession is not working even in the nominal sense. These periods are mainly spent sitting around moaning about agents and slagging off their more successful colleagues – which is exactly what they do when they are in work (see above). A good actor should make this fine line between their activities when supposedly working at their job and when they are at rest so fine as to be largely pointless.

One last thing. Because the style is now for more realistic acting on TV and the stage, actors are getting away with doing even less work. At least in the days of blustering darlings you could see them making the effort. They would declaim and gesture and emote. Now it's all silences and glances; half the time you can't even tell if they're acting.

And that is, let's face it, the whole point of being an actor. ☙

I love it when I read interviews where actors go on about their "work", their "craft" and their "business". I love it, then I scoff

THE EVENING STROLLERS' SOCIETY

If you are a *flâneur*, a city wanderer, then read
Anna Pharoah's history of your spiritual ancestors

As its title would suggest, this society was founded by people, who, of an evening, might take a leisurely stroll. It first gained notoriety in the 1800s, just after the introduction of lampposts.

Evidence has been uncovered suggesting that strollers used to express lightness-of-mood by taking hold of a lamppost shaft and using it to pivot a 360-degree turn, before continuing onward.

The consequence of this activity over time was that lampposts became noticeably thinner and shinier in places.

Have a look next time you see an old lamppost.

Despite the Strollers' exuberance, one of its leading members, Dr. Sloan-Downe saw fit to set a strolling speed limit, at three miles per hour, where it has remained since 1882.

Electricity wrought massive changes in the nuances of evening strolls, a subject that has been written about extensively in the epic book *Noctambulation Through the Ages*. Despite the transformation, once a year, unfailingly, The Evening Strollers' Society awards The Stroll-Worthy Sign to a lamppost deemed to cast an exceptional spot of light.

In The Great Pavement Narrowing of 1918, many Strollers risked their lives in a brief period of exertion. They lead a bloody campaign, which resulted in the minimum unobstructed width requirement for pavements being set at 1.8 meters, rather than 1.7. This was the Strollers' most marked achievement, but there was trouble ahead.

The Dawdling Act of 1953, required strollers to carry a permit and stipulated that only those with five years strolling experience were entitled to one. This forced strolling to become an underground activity and wasn't helped by the fact that during the 1980s a new kind of street revelling appeared on the scene, in the form of the more virulent Pimp Roll, which has now replaced strolling completely, in some regions. 🐌

THE TRUTH

Brian Dean continues his regular column with some revealing statistics about our working lives.
Illustrations by Chlöe King

DEADLINE

People Hate Work

In 2001, the UK government announced plans for a "work first" culture. Ministers spoke of how work "holds communities together" and "gives life meaning". Meanwhile, back in the real world...

• In 2002, the Work Foundation reported that "job satisfaction has plummeted", and that so-called "high performance" management techniques made workers deeply unhappy and failed to raise output.

• In January 2004, a marketing director at Prudential was reported as saying: "Our research shows that an alarming number of people appear to be unhappy in their employment and unfulfilled by their work". A British Social Attitudes survey revealed that six in ten British workers are unhappy in their jobs, with a majority reporting feelings of insecurity, stress, pointlessness, exhaustion and inadequate income.

• A Samaritans survey found that jobs are the single biggest cause of stress and that the link between work and suicide is likely to be underestimated. In Japan, around 5% of all suicides are "company related" and suicide is an official, compensated work-related condition.

• In a pathetic attempt to raise worker morale, employers are giving high-sounding titles to mundane jobs. The recruitment company, Reed, noticed these examples:

• Technical Sanitation Assistant *(toilet cleaner)*
• Optical Illuminator Enhancer *(window cleaner)*
• Head of Verbal Communications *(receptionist)*
• Senior Corporate Events Manager *(secretary)*

(Sources: Work Foundation, April 2002; *Christian Science Monitor*, 12 Jan 2004; BSA survey; The Samaritans '*Stressed Out*', May 2003; *Hazards* magazine factsheet 83, 2003; *The Japan Times*, 10 May 2003; Study by Reed, March 2002)

Long Working Hours

Working hours have risen in the last twenty years, on average, for UK full-time workers (as shown by the UK Labour Force Survey). This reverses a 150-year trend of declining working hours.

UK governments have known for decades that long hours are economically counter-productive. A 1916 Home Office report, *Industrial Fatigue*, noted that output "is lowered by the working of overtime. The diminution is often so great that the total daily output is less when overtime is worked than when it is suspended. Thus overtime defeats its own object." The UK government has admitted a "sharp increase" in excessive working hours. DTI research found that one in six employees now work more than sixty hours a week.. Full-time employees in the UK work the longest hours in Europe. The average for full-timers in the UK is 43.5 hours per week. In France it's 38.2 and in Germany 39.9, yet both are more productive than the UK.

• According to an ICM poll, one in five UK workers never take a lunch-break. And 57% of workers take a break of less than thirty minutes (thirty minutes is the legal minimum).

• A May 2003 British Medical Association survey found that 77% of consultants work more than fifty hours a week for the NHS, and 46% more than sixty hours.

• Each year employees are giving £23 billion in free labour to their bosses, according to the TUC. The union organisation has designated February 27th as "Work Your Proper Hours Day", after calculating that this is the day when the average worker who does unpaid overtime stops working for free.

(Sources: UK Labour Force Survey, *Historical Supplement and Quarterly Supplement*, Autumn 1999; *Hazards* magazine factsheet 78, 2002; *Guardian*, 30 Aug 2002; *TUC* online, tuc.org.uk; *ICM* poll quoted by *jobserve.com*; *Hazards* magazine factsheet 83, 2003; Press Association, Feb 26 2004)

Death By Work

People with stressful jobs are twice as likely to die from heart disease, according to a 2002 study in the British Medical Journal.

People who work over forty-eight hours per week have double the risk of heart disease, according to a 1996 UK government report. Long-term job strain is worse for your heart than gaining 40lbs in weight or aging thirty years, according to a 2003 US study.

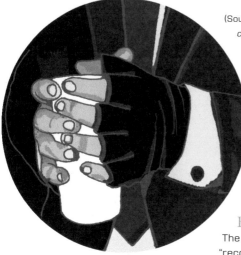

(Sources: *Work stress and risk of cardiovascular mortality... British Medical Journal*, 19 Oct 2002; *The Money Programme*, BBC2, 11 Feb 1996; *Life course exposure to job strain..., American Journal of Epidemiology*, 2003; *UN International Labor Organisation SafeWork programme*, April 2002; *PCS* survey, May 2003; *Hazards* magazine no. 81; *BBC News Online*, 7 Nov 2001; *British Dental Health Foundation*, 27 Jan 2000)

Work is Not a Cure for Poverty

The number of people in work is at "record levels" according to the UK government. Meanwhile, official UK figures show 22% of people living in poverty, compared to 13% in 1979.

47% of employees have wages that, on their own, are insufficient to avoid poverty.

42% of employees rely on means other than their own wages to avoid poverty. In the 1970s and 1980s, around 4% of low-paid employees lived in poverty. Currently, 14% of low-paid employees live in poverty. (5% of all employees now live in poverty). Since the early 1970s GDP (national income) has doubled, but in real terms (ie allowing for inflation) the bottom 10% of jobs pay less now than in 1970. The minimum wage would have to be around £6.50 per hour to bring low-pay up to the 1970 level. Meanwhile, in America, 40% of those served in soup kitchens have jobs. Nearly a fifth of all homeless people in the USA are employed in jobs.

(Sources: Government DWP press release, Nov 2004; poverty.org.uk; Joseph Rowntree Foundation study, Nov 2004; *Guardian*, 14 Jun 2002; National Coalition for the Homeless, 1997)

- Work kills more than war. Approximately two million workers die annually due to occupational injuries and illnesses, according to a United Nations report. This is more than double the figure for deaths from warfare (650,000 deaths per year). Work kills more people than alcohol and drugs together.
- 82% of workers at the Department for Work and Pensions have suffered ill health as a result of pressure of work, according to a 2003 survey.
- The Health and Safety Executive reports that the number of people suffering from work-related stress has more than doubled since 1990. BBC News quotes the International Stress Management Association as saying: "Each year we conduct research into stress and each year the figure just keeps on getting worse."
- Rising stress at work is causing increasing numbers of young professionals to grind their teeth while they sleep, according to the British Dental Health Foundation.

The Future as Previously Predicted

In the late 1700s, Benjamin Franklin predicted we'd soon work a 4-hour week. George Bernard Shaw predicted we'd work a 2-hour day by 2000.

In 1933, the US Senate passed a bill for an official 30-hour work week. (President Roosevelt killed it.)

In 1935, W.K. Kellogg introduced a scheme to cut 2 hours from the working day, yet pay the same wages. It was cost-effective – morale and productivity rose; accident and insurance rates fell. In 1956, Richard Nixon predicted a 4-day work week in the "not too distant future".

In 1965, a US Senate subcommittee predicted a 22-hour work week by 1985, 14 hours by 2000.

• In the 1960s, Paul and Percival Goodman estimated that just 5% of the work being done would satisfy our food, clothing and shelter needs.

In 1981, Buckminster Fuller claimed that 70% of US jobs were unnecessary: "inspectors of inspectors, reunderwriters of insurance reinsurers, Obnoxico promoters, spies and counterspies..."

(*Sources: Carl Honoré, In Praise of Slow*; John de Graaf, *Affluenza*; Jeremy Rifkin, *The End of Work*; Bob Black, *The Abolition of Work*; Buckminster Fuller, *Critical Path*)
Brian Dean runs anxietyculture.com

CRAP JOBS

Ben Perry doesn't give a shit anymore

SECURITY NOTICE

THIS PROPERTY IS PROTECTED BY ELECTRONIC SURVEILLANCE

SECURITY GUARD

I once worked for a major toy retailer as a security guard. I spent many happy months leaning against various surfaces watching thousands of pounds worth of stock being shoplifted and not doing a damn thing to stop it. My best day came when, whilst playing hangman with the customer service girl, I noticed a six year old child ride a stolen bicycle straight out of the door followed by her anxious looking parents. As they hurried to the exit, I gave them a smile and a little wave. Perhaps my actions would have been different if the slave-driving corporate Nazis who ran the store had paid me more than three quid an hour to protect their overpriced wares.

THE IDLE COOK

SUCKLING PIG by Rowley Leigh

In Bairrada, a nondescript Portugese village in the hinterland between Lisbon and Porto, there is little sign of human habitation. Every building appears to be a restaurant, most of them huge joints capable of seating at least 300, with car parks the size of sports fields. And every one of these establishments has the same *raison d'etre*, which is the cooking and eating of suckling pigs. We entered one establishment via what appeared to be a kind of kitchen that consisted of little more than a row of eight very large brick built ovens, each large enough to accommodate four pigs. We blundered past and entered a huge dining room; families of twelve or twenty, old couples, coachloads of blokey males, courting couples packed the place. It was like La Coupole in Lancashire. It was only in a third, hangar like space that we were accommodated, and presented with a long and complicated menu that, along with everyone else in the restaurant, we ignored and proceeded to eat a large quantity of the crispest and most succulent meat served on cheap steel platters, accompanied by bowls of chips, an excuse for a salad and a pungent local *vino tinto*.

Porcelet A L'Occitane

- Clean out the pig by means of a short incision in the belly. Bone out the pig, leaving the leg bones in position. Season the interior with salt, pepper and mixed spice and rinse out with brandy.

- Prepare the stuffing. Slice the liver, the hearts and the kidneys and seize them briefly with butter, together with 200 grams of blanched lamb sweetbreads. Leave to cool. Stew two finely chopped onions in butter until soft and add a cupful of mushroom *duxelles*, three finely chopped cloves of garlic and a quarter a bottle of Jurancon wine. Reduce this mixture and moisten with a quarter litre of rich veal stock. Blanch 200 grams of diced bacon rinds and add to the sauce, together with thirty stoned and blanched green olives. Cool in turn. Mix together the sauce, the offal together with two handfuls of fresh bread-crumbs, half a kilo of sausage meat, two handfuls of chopped parsley and a glass of brandy. Season well with salt and pepper before placing this mixture in the cavity of the pig. Sew up the interior and marinade the pig in a marinade of olive oil, white wine, onions carrots and pot herbs overnight.

- The next day, place the piglet on a rack of an oven tray and cover with thin slices of pork fat, with the marinade in the tray beneath. Roast in a slow oven for five hours, basting occasionally with a mixture of olive oil, brandy and white wine. Allow to rest for half an hour before taking to the table, surrounded by little pork *crepinettes*, black puddings and whole roast onions. The cooking juices should be strained and served alongside. A purée of celeriac and potato is a traditional and efficacious accompaniment. ◉

LIBRARIES

THE MARX MEMORIAL

Edward Sage tells the story of Clerkenwell's Marx Memorial Library, home of radical thought since 1872

The Marx Memorial Library is housed in 37a Clerkenwell Green, a striking pale-green structure designed by James Steer for the British Charity School in 1738. 37a's connection with radical politics began in 1872 when the London Patriotic Club met there. The Club, which was often visited by Engels and Eleanor Marx, supported trade unionism, universal suffrage and republicanism. In 1892 the Social Democratic Federation's Twentieth Century Press moved in. With the aid of William Morris, who contributed £50 towards the first year's rent, they published some of the earliest editions of Marx and Engels' writings. While exiled in London from 1902-03, Lenin used one of the small first-floor offices to produce *Iskra* (The Spark), the Russian Social Democratic newspaper.

1933 saw the 50th anniversary of Karl Marx's death, and delegates from the London labour movement gathered in 37a to plan a permanent memorial to him. With the Nazis burning books in Germany, a library was thought to be the most fitting commemoration; the Marx Memorial Library was established there that same year.

In 1934 Jack Hastings, pupil of Diego Rivera, painted a mural on the wall of the lecture room. The painting was entitled "The worker of the future upsetting the economic chaos of the present", but when the library moved upstairs it was concealed by books and forgotten for forty years. The restoration became the subject of a 1991 television programme entitled "Marx on the Wall".

The library's lending section contains some 20,000 volumes relating to Marxism, Socialism, history, economics, biographies and literature. They possess the only complete sets of the *Daily Worker* and *Morning Star* newspapers. Their International Brigade archive and

library contains arguably the world's most comprehensive collection on the Spanish Civil War.

In July 2004 the Clerkenwell Literary Festival held events there, featuring Keith Allen, Robert Newman, Stewart Home and Alex James. ◉

THE WIT AND WISDOM OF
AUBERON WAUGH

Paul Hamilton rounds up some choice excerpts from the writing
of the truculent journalist

April 21, 1973

Sometimes I worry about our children. They sit watching odious, patronising rubbish like *Blue Peter* week after week, and when a chance comes to get their own back they do nothing about it. The Blue Peter Old Folks Appeal for treasures from the attic was a golden opportunity for the nation's kiddies to show their satirical mettle. My own attics are a treasury of rotting mattresses, fossilised dog shit, old sets of false teeth, dead bats, broken light bulbs and old plastic potties. If only I had heard of the Appeal in time, it would have been the work of a moment to send the entire contents round to *Blue Peter*. If enough people had done the same we might have put a stop to this sentimental filth which is perverting the moral awareness of an entire generation.

November 18, 1973

I always try to be in the House of Commons when the Minister for Posts and Telecommunications is answering his Parliamentary Questions. Today Sir John Eden revealed that the number of incidents involving vandalism of telephone kiosks declined from 29,000 in the quarter ending June 1972 to 20,000 for the same period this year. Whatever the reason for this sad decline I hope it does not mean that the British public is losing its taste for breaking things. There was a time when the sound of breaking glass was a pleasure restricted to richer members of society who could afford it. One of the most agreeable features of social progress in our time is the way the Government has built these kiosks for even the humblest members of society to try their hand. The pleasures of telephoning are obviously much over-rated, but various people have suggested that destroying these kiosks is a mistake from the point of view of members of the lower class who have no telephone themselves and wish to summon help in the event of an emergency – suddenly finding themselves being murdered, for instance, or on fire. On the other hand, they are not accustomed to these luxuries, and I should have thought that by now they must have found some more dignified way of drawing attention to their distress. I confess I can never see an unvandalised telephone kiosk as anything but a challenge.

May 15, 1974

I am sure I was right to refuse to put up the £65,000 needed to get the engineers back to work. There is a certain amount of entertainment to be derived from the spectacle of other people working, it is true, but surely not £65,000-worth. For that sort of money I could invite the whole county [of Somerset] to lunch with a brass band and a special performance of Iolanthe or Yeomen of the Guard thrown in.

If only Grocer [Edward Heath] was still in charge, there would have been a General Strike. Many of us could have our first opportunity to drive a bus or hit some workers on the head with a truncheon. [...] Until Grocer is replaced by lovely, oyster-eyed Willie Whitelaw we must leave the government of our country to Hugh Scanlon, and start worrying seriously about whether Mrs Scanlon wears frilly knickers or plain ones. The Central office of Information, which I have been telephoning daily for the last eight weeks, has still to make an announcement on this important matter. Until it does, I think we must decide that democracy in this country has been superceded by the dictatorship of the proletariat in its customarily brutal and repressive forms.

August 6, 1975

Winston S. Churchill Jr., the former Boy Scout and Member for Stretford, reveals the activities of badge-wearing Communists in the BBC's Portuguese Service, but where on earth does he want these people to be?

One of the pleasanter aspects of English life has always been that these Communist badgers are concentrated in various recognisable areas of boredom – the BBC, the House of Commons, Times Newspapers Ltd., and the trade union movement – where sensible people can easily avoid them. The only result of Churchill's silly behaviour must be to disperse them. [...] This tiresome young man threatens to become as great a nuisance as his loathsome grandfather, the war criminal, mass murderer and persecutor of P.G. Wodehouse.

July 28, 1976

"BRAINS OF BRITAIN QUIT IN DROVES" says the front page of the *Sunday Express*. I nearly sent them a telegram of reassurance, that I'm only away for a week. But they are worried about doctors and scientists and suchlike.

If the *Sunday Express* hopes to panic our rulers into doing something about it, they are making a big mistake. Union bosses would only be too delighted if nobody remained in this country who had an IQ of more than fifteen.

Then the handful of crafty, crooked union leaders left behind could appoint each other Lords Warden of the Cinque Ports, Keepers of the Privy Purse, Knights of the Garter – while the sottish masses gape open-mouthed at them and cheer obsequiously whenever they are told to do so. I don't care. I shall stay behind and sneer at them even if it means having to eat tinned spaghetti on toast for the rest of my life.

November 24, 1977

Perhaps it is too late to do anything about growing squashy apples for old people. It appears they are all going to be burned to death as a result of the firemen's strike. Old people and children will be the first to burn according to the Home Secretary, whose name I failed to catch. This may explain why the strike is so popular. At times it has seemed that I was the only person who realised how much the English hate children and old people, but nobody can doubt it now as they see striking firemen showered with gifts of money, pheasants and warm winter clothing. My only dread is in case any of our beloved workers are burned. They are especially vulnerable living in their picturesque high-rise tower blocks where the lifts are out of order and the stairways choked with debris as the result of other strikes.

Even if it is true, as Wedgwood Benn argues, that the "workers" are now an expensive anachronism this doesn't stop us from being sentimental about them. I particularly like the way they talk with cigarettes in their mouths.

April 12, 1978

I am growing very upset by these photographs of Kate Bush. She may be magical, beautiful, wondrous, breathtaking, but I don't suppose she is available. Many girls of that age, when one enquires, already have some pimply swain in tow; if they don't, it usually means they are heavily involved in transactional analysis or some such rubbish.

The whole idea of advertising her in this way is silly and misguided. But there are wondrous, breathtaking things to be done to her face with a marker pen in the quiet moments of the evening on London's Underground.

August 28, 1979

"Did Fulham win on Saturday?" These words – the first spoken by 52-year-old football fan Keith Castle after his £70,000 heart transplant – will reverberate around the world, says Glenda Slag, the First Lady of Greek Street.

But one can't help asking oneself, if that is the limit of Keith Castle's intellectual curiosity, whether it was really worth the trouble to keep him alive. He must have heard the results of plenty of matches in his time. Was it really worth £70,000 of public money to let this sickly, retired gentleman learn one more football result?

on Super Stink Bombs. What this foolish man does not realise is that the smaller stink bomb is ineffective out of doors. It may be perfectly all right for teenage snogging parties, editorial conferences and progressive church meetings, but it is perfectly useless at somewhere like Wimbledon.

The Government claims that at close quarters the Pong bomb may have an adverse effect on Old Age Pensioners or some such rubbish, but almost anything has an adverse effect on Old Age Pensioners at close quarters. It looks as if another traditional British freedom will be taken away without a whimper of dissent from the cowed masses.

July 5, 1980

"Your average stink-bomb will not be affected," says a terrible man called Mr John Henley, managing director of Mad Hatter Novelty Distributors of Boreham Wood, Hants, when I telephone to enquire about the Government's new prohibition

September 21, 1981

Last night, unable to sleep for worrying about badgers, I watched Glenda Jackson in Ken Russell's *The Music Lovers*. Hideous woman, dreadful film. One can't really blame Tchaikovsky for preferring boys. ◉

D05513r   *About you*

Please fill in this form with a Medium 500μ Black Rollerball fineliner in BLOCK CAPITALS using a piece of lined paper underneath as a guide. You must answer ALL the questions. If you do not know the answer to a question you must think about it for a bit and make a pot of tea. The judge's decision is final.

Tick boxes (☐) should be filled in with a jaunty tick thus: ✔

Do NOT fill with a diagonal cross: ✖ This isn't the Football Pools.

Your name   ☐

Do you have a partner?   **Yes** ☐   Please send us some of their skin.

                                  No ☐   Please tell us about your inability to
                                              trust others on a separate sheet.

May we look in your dustbin? **Yes** ☐   We will return in a suspicious-looking
We need to do this in order to   boiler suit.
freak you out.

Do you have children?   **No** ☐   What have you done with them?

                                  Yes ☐   Please answer the following question:

What is their total weight in bushels? ☐
We need to know this in order to cause
you as much trouble as possible.

Would you care for an older relative? **No** ☐   Thanks, I've just put one out.

                                           Yes ☐ Please answer the following:

Please estimate their calorific value. ☐

Do you find this form confusing in any way? ☐   **9.** See 12 Across (4,3)

About your partner

Your name

That's a pretty name.

"What the fuck have you done with my tax records?"

The Department of Social Scrutiny is pleased to announce publication of *Britain - A User's Guide* by Ian Vince October 7 as well as the second imprint of *What the Fuck Have You Done With My Tax Records?* in line with a European ruling on Equality of Incompetence.
Britain - A User's Guide is published by Boxtree: ISBN 0752225987.

CRAP TOWNS

There may be dissent when it comes to Bridgewater's status as a crap town but no-one came to Taunton's defence

TAUNTON

Population: 102.300 **Unemployment:** 2.4% **Violent Crime (per 1,000 population):** 11
Famous residents: Charles Dance, Jenny Agutter

Taunton was once a small prosperous market town surrounded by beautiful, rolling countryside. Then the developers arrived. Surrounded by an overturned sick bucket of superstores, business parks and identikit starter homes, Taunton is now a place with its head stuck firmly in a trough of pigswill. Like many a town in middle England, it's town centre has been wilfully mugged by property developers and town planners who, over the past fifteen years, have combined to create a truly epic blandness. About ten years ago, the council introduced talking litterbins and in 2003 some bloke drowned trying to retrieve his mobile phone from a drain. Need I say any more about Taunton's collective pointlessness and stupidity?
Matt Knight

40 YEAR RESIDENT WRITES

Taunton is as forward thinking as the Monmouth rebellion and as successful. Every Saturday and Sunday morning trash cans lay upturned alongside vandalised bollards while numerous life belts and smashed park benches float uselessly in the river. Taunton's "revamped" town centre is already falling apart and through lack of funding cannot be repaired in the same materials, the CCTV system is a complete waste of time and the vandals still vandalise. Even the local Police force has neither the will nor the manpower to stop even the pavement cyclists.

There have been many enterprising people who've set up businesses in Taunton only to find the apathetic attitude of the local population utterly crippling. In fact the only businesses that thrive are the pubs and the glaziers, whose customers seem to destroy and then repair the town on a depressingly monotonous basis.
Jim Laws ☙

CRAP TOWN TRIVIA

After the publication of an article in the *Western Daily Press* about Crap Towns the email subject line, "What about Taunton?" appeared sixty-three times in the Idler's inbox.

THE IDLER QUESTIONNAIRE:
TERRY HALL

What time do you get up?
Eight or eleven am

Do you leap up or lie slumbering? My head leaps out, my body has a lie-in...

Do you smoke and drink, and if so, how much?
Smoke too much, don't drink enough.

How many hours work do you put in on an average day?
Between two and twenty.

Do you take holidays?
Not if I can help it.

Where do you live?
London.

Where do you work?
Everywhere but Turkey.

Where do you think?
Alone in my car.

What are your three greatest pleasures?
Man United, wife, kids...

Do you like money?
No, but it seems to be fond of me.

Are you happy?
You tell me.

How many hours do you sleep at night/day?
Six hours at night, fifteen minutes a day.

What are you reading?
This questionnaire.

If it came to the crunch, would you choose money or art?
Art if I could afford it.

What have you been thinking about?
United's midfield problems.

Who are your heroes?
George Best, Bernard Manning, Patti Smith.

Any advice for young people?
Grow old as quickly as you can.

Do you like to go a-wandering?
Not if it means leaving the house.

What is paradise?
Old Trafford on a wet Wednesday night. ☻

CRAP TOWNS USA

DULUTH, MINNESOTA

Population: 87,000 **Unemployment:** 3.8% **Famous residents:** Are you joking?

A sad, declining industrial wasteland in the arctic northern mid-west. The buildings are linked by sky bridges, to save the residents the despair of having to go outside and see their city for what it is – a crumbling shell of its former horrific self. Duluth is Middlesbrough without the pizzazz.
James Davis ☻

THE FEAR OF THE LORD IS THE BEGINNING OF WISDOM!

GWYN

MASQUERADE

Paul Slade on a 1970s treasure hunt that led to madness. Illustration by Anthony Haythornthwaite

When Kit Williams published his 1979 puzzle book *Masquerade*, nearly two million readers joined the treasure hunt it inspired. But only Richard Dale went so far as to sacrifice his sanity in the pursuit of Williams' golden hare.

Dale first saw *Masquerade* at a friend's house near his Philadelphia home on August 24, 1981. He was immediately captivated by the puzzle, persuaded his friend to give him the book, and set about researching its solution. Williams had specified that the prize medallion was buried somewhere in the UK, so Dale began with the only source of British maps he had available: a copy of the London *A-Z*. He rapidly concluded that the hare was buried near West Middlesex Drainage Works in Hounslow and booked himself a cheap flight across the Atlantic.

By the time Dale boarded his plane, Williams was already becoming accustomed to obsessive *Masquerade* fans and their bizarre behaviour. At the height of the craze he received up to 200 letters a day, including one from a Swiss reader who used his family's savings to fund a trip to Cornwall where he had climbed down what he believed was a crucial cliff face and been cut off by the incoming tide. Every week produced a new batch of muddy lunatics at Williams' Gloucestershire cottage, waving muck-encrusted shovels at him and babbling excitedly about the hare's supposed location.

"The world went crazy," he later recalled. "People seized on everything I had put in the book and lots of things I hadn't. One poor woman had her garden invaded when people spotted the topiary hare in the aerial view of Tewkesbury." (1)

The Tewkesbury picture was just one of fifteen Williams paintings in the book, each one embedded with a host of visual, mathematical and linguistic clues. Anyone who solved all the clues correctly—and managed to avoid Williams' fiendish red herrings—would produce a nineteen word phrase telling them where the prize was buried. The medallion itself, also made by Williams, was cast from 18 carat gold and inlaid with precious stones. It was valued at £5,000 in 1979 (about £15,500 today).

Despite the medallion's financial value, most of the book's followers were driven more by intellectual curiosity than simple greed. None were more determined to solve the puzzle than Dale. When he arrived in Hounslow, he searched the area for a while, and then settled on a drain cover in Oak Lane which seemed significant. He prised it up and fished out a five and a half inch ceramic plug from the drain wall. Dale

> Dale decided that the extra task he was expected to perform must involve toilet paper

pocketed the plug and took it back to his hotel room. Once he'd cleaned it up, he decided he could see the initials "KW" (for "Kit Williams") on its surface.

Next morning, when Jonathan Cape, Williams' publisher, opened its doors for business Dale was already waiting on the step. He explained his discovery to three different people there, all of whom told him as gently as possible that he was mistaken. Convinced they were lying, Dale called *The Sunday Times* instead, where three journalists agreed to meet with him. Unfortunately, they proved just as unable to detect the "KW" initials as the Jonathan Cape people had been, and Dale found himself back on the street.

He was still convinced he was right, but felt sure now that he was being asked to pass some additional test before his victory could be acknowledged. He began to see everything around him – a London cabbie's casual conversation, a scuffle in the

local pub - as vital clues to the conspiracy. Back home in Philadelphia, he matched his own experiences to Lewis Carroll's *Alice in Wonderland*, and allocated roles from the book to his own tormentors. Any fresh information which contradicted his convictions was simply evidence of how cunning his enemies could be in laying a false trail.

"I convinced myself that Kit Williams' book was a media masquerade," he later said. "Performed in print, on television, involving perhaps hundreds of people in every country where the book has been published. The biggest masquerade in the history of mankind." (2)

And then, on March 14, 1982, Williams announced that the real hare medallion had been found not in Hounslow, but in Ampthill, near Bedford.

Williams received the letter giving this solution on February 19, 1982. It contained a crude, child-like sketch showing Catherine of Aragon's cross in Ampthill Park. The sender, who called himself Ken Thomas, had added a shadow extending northward from the cross and marked that shadow's tip as the place where the hare was buried. He made no pretence to have solved the book's clues in any detail, but said he had been led to Ampthill by the simple fact that he knew Williams used to live nearby, and had stumbled on the exact location when his dog stopped to pee on a standing stone near the cross.

This may not have been the most satisfying solution *Masquerade*'s creator could have asked for, but there was no denying Thomas had got the right location. Williams called the number given in the letter and told him so. Five days later, Thomas and a friend returned to the site and dug up the hare in its earthenware casket.

When he heard the news, Dale assumed this development was just one more twist in the global conspiracy against him. His suspicions were further raised when Thomas insisted on hiding behind frosted glass for his one and only television appearance. Were Williams and his cronies indirectly acknowledging that the hunt was over, but substituting an actor for Dale? Could "Thomas" even be Williams himself?

For reasons only he knows, Dale decided that the extra task he was expected to perform must involve toilet paper. He mailed Williams a roll from Philadelphia and then, concluding this had probably been stolen by UK postal workers, followed it up with a long strip on which he had written the entire Sermon on the Mount. Finally, he decided that Agatha Christie must be behind the whole cruel plot. After all, she had died in 1976, the year Williams began work on *Masquerade*, and left quite enough money in her estate to fund the whole scheme. Who better than a detective novelist to dream up the infinite complexities involved?

In 1983, Dale finally agreed to seek psychiatric help. It would be another five years before the true story behind Ken Thomas' find emerged.

On December 11, 1988, *The Sunday Times* reported that Thomas' real name was Dugald Thompson. back in 1982, the story added, Thompson had worked with a business partner called John Guard. Veronica Robertson, who had been Williams' girlfriend when he conceived *Masquerade*, was by then living with Guard. Robertson told *The Sunday Times* that she had led Thompson and Guard to the medallion's hiding place in return for a promise that any funds raised from its sale would go to an animal rights group. Thompson had used a false name and insisted that his appearance be disguised on TV because he wanted to conceal his links with Guard and, through him, with Williams' old girlfriend.

Once all the 1982 publicity had passed, Thompson used the hare medallion as security to set up a computer games company called Haresoft, which later went bust. Haresoft's liquidators auctioned the medallion at Sotheby's in December 1988, where it fetched £31,900 from a mystery bidder. Williams tried to buy the medallion himself at the same auction, but was forced to drop out when the price reached £6,000. No-one knows who owns it now.

One rather sad footnote remains. Just a month after Williams had received the Ken Thomas letter, he heard from Mike Barker and John Rousseau,

two Lancashire physics teachers. Unlike Thompson and Guard, the two teachers had solved Williams' puzzle in every particular. Their letter gave a perfect step-by-step account of how they had reached Williams' still-secret key: "Catherine's, long finger, over, shadows, earth. Buried, yellow, amulet, midday, points, the, hour. In, light of equinox, look you". They had also spotted the key's confirming acrostic: "Close by ampthill".

Barker and Rousseau had first dug at Catherine's cross as early as February 18, 1982, but managed to miss the hare. They filled the hole in carelessly and returned home, deciding to wait for the crucial Spring equinox on March 21 before they tried again. But the Ken Thomas letter was already in the post by February 18, and would reach Williams the next day. Indeed, it may have been the traces left by Barker and Rousseau on an earlier reconnaissance mission which prompted "Thomas" to write when he did. The two teachers had stuck to *Masquerade*'s spirit in a way which Thompson and Guard certainly did not, but they lost out all the same. 🐚

1) Masquerade by Kit Williams (1979).
2) Quest For The Golden Hare, by Bamber Gascoigne (1983).

For a full explanation of Masquerade's solution, see www.bunnyears.net/kitwilliams

BRITISH QUIZZES RANKED BY CLASS

Devised by Greg Rowland and Matthew De Abaitua

The quiz show has been a favourite of this country for many years and reflects our national obsession with social class. Know your favourite quiz show, know your place.

UPPER MIDDLE CLASS

Round Britain Quiz
Presented on Radio 4 by Robert Robertson, this is the only remaining quiz show where the contestants are referred to by their surnames; like a summer's evening surveying one's estate in the company of retired civil servants.

Ask The Family
Another entry in Robert Robertson's one man campaign to posh up the quiz show. Families were arranged by their matching pervert-sicko 1970s eye-glasses, their soulless twig-dry exterior hiding a seething mass of bitterness and dark S&M fantasies.

MIDDLE MIDDLE CLASS

University Challenge
While the opening up of higher education to the lower orders has led to decline in the status of this programme, its continuing refusal to have any truck with gaudy prizes make it solidly bourgeois.

Countdown
It is Richard Whiteley's squirming with embarrassment at presenting a quiz show that makes this a cut above the rest. Plus the fact that it is about letters and numbers, and therefore ostensibly, though not actually, "clever".

Fifteen-to-one
Like the army, there are too many thickies making up the numbers. The Lighting Crew used the code-name "'he Vegetables" to refer to the contestants. Fact.

LOWER MIDDLE CLASS

Who Wants To Be A Millionaire
The classes unite around suburban avarice. Chris Tarrant's balls smell of pork. Fact.

Krypton Factor
A Northern TV show, so its aspirations are a grim masquerade — middle management gone Nietzsche. No one ever looked like Superman, or even had the slightest vestige of Superpowers. Typical Northern English pathetic self-aggrandisement.

CLASS

UPPER WORKING CLASS

Generation Game
In which middle class contestants face working class challenges. The conveyor belt, that symbol of factory drudgery, wheeled out for cheap posh laughs. Almost as much fun as watching the decimation of British Manufacturing Industry in the 1980s.

321
Its poetry was mere doggerel. Angry young men tormented their dumb peers with the vile verse of autodidacts. Featuring the least funny "comedy sketches" ever to grace TV. No-one in Yorkshire has ever said anything funny ever.

MIDDLE WORKING CLASS

Family Fortunes
The stultifying conformity of lower middle is paraded as a virtue. Contestants are rewarded for the mundanity of their answers. Distinctiveness is punished with an electronic UGH-UGHHHH.

Play Your Cards Right
The contestants of *Family Fortunes* before they had kids. The Dolly Birds gave the show the air of a swingers party in which the contestants were first-timers. Brucie was the old goat libertine, a man who appetites could no longer be slaked by anything less than a four-way involving giant playing cards.

LOWER WORKING CLASS

The Price Is Right
The first show bold enough to strip the lower orders of their dignity and reduce us all to the level of insects. The first time US-style audience "whooping" was heard on British T.V.

Wheel Of Fortune
Not since the ancient civilisation of Sumeria have people clapped a spinning wheel.

Bullseye
In which the casual friendships of the pub replace the wholesome bond of the family. Pre-*Kilroy*, *Bullseye* was the last time working class people were shy on television. The presenter's ineptitude has given rise to the phrase "Bowenesque" to signify a grim working-class attempt at jollity at inappropriate moments.

UNDERCLASS

Celebrity Battleships
Or just about any multichannel quiz offering where the words "text us the answer now or else we will not meet the grossly inflated expectations of our business plan" appear on the screen. A City of the Dead for the Information Age.

CRAP HOLIDAYS

Rik Denana gets stuck between a hippy and an airforce base

FINDHORN

discovered the greenhouse was, in fact, "A Living Toilet." Eco-toilet my arse. It was just a big hole in the ground, filled with hippy excrement and sawdust, covered by a polytunnel. When the wind blew in from the east (all day every day) it was like staying in a shit-filled turbine on the coast of hell.

After a sleepless first night filled with nightmares (involving fighter planes, burning turds and my tent) I headed for the commune reception area to sign in. The commune actively encouraged visitors. In exchange for a morning's work you were fed and grinned at by purple-trouser wearing, middle-aged women recovering from nervous breakdowns. You may ask what the hell I was doing there. It's a bloody good question. I blame a particularly nasty break-up and too many Sundays watching the *Heaven and Earth Show*.

I opted to work in the garden and headed for the rows and rows of vegetables on the other side of the grounds. There were six of

Looking back, going camping in Scotland for a holiday was perhaps a bit naive, but this wasn't any ordinary campsite. It was a campsite beside a hippy commune in a place called Findhorn, which sits directly next to an American Airforce base on the edge of the Moray Firth.

I felt slightly bewildered as I pitched my tent while a flock of B52 bombers lifted off the runway that ended a few hundred yards from where I was hoping to sleep, but was intrigued by the enormous greenhouse that lay a few yards away. This intrigue gave way to stomach churning panic when I

us in all but I was the only volunteer. The lady who ran the garden was an attractive American woman who spoke to us as though we were a bunch of five year olds. She instructed us to hold hands in a circle so we could "bless the garden" before asking each of us in turn to imagine that we were a tree. After imagining this for a while, and swaying from side to side humming, she asked us to explain to the group which kind of tree we were. After confessing that she was an oak tree, the other three turned out to be pine trees and then I too confirmed that I was an oak tree. The American woman grinned at me and asked if anyone needed my help with their morning's work. I looked around the circle expecting some kind of response but they all just stared at their feet looking full of guilt. She turned back to me and smiled nervously, "That's great! I need help! Please will you come and help me?"

The other four slipped off and I found myself being led around the garden with a hoe in my hand. Before starting work she held my wrists, looked into my eyes and said, "Don't forget to thank the weeds when you pull them out of the ground. Thank them for doing their job in the garden, then place them carefully over there," she pointed at a compost heap, "then they can live again in the earth." I had been idly nursing the vague hope of a shag and a decent bed for the night, but she was clearly completely and utterly insane.

I had intended to stay for a week, but then the rain came. I wept in my tent for the next twelve hours, tortured by the neverending drone of warplanes and the feverish cold of a Scottish summer night. The next morning I picked up the remaining pieces of my fractured spirit and left. ☯

The Idler Book of Crap Holidays is published by Transworld in October 2005

IDLE PLEASURES: SUNBEAMS

IN A DAZE, you climb down the stairs on a summer morning. All the curtains in the room below are closed except one. A sunbeam cuts through the darkness and on to the blue carpet – dust flecked in its refracting light. Your bare feet lead you to its edge. You dip your toe into the warmth before submerging your entire foot. A line of glowing light draws itself across your ankle, restoring you with its gentle affection. Gradually you get on your knees and immerse yourself into the light completely. You curl up into a ball and go back to sleep. ☯   DAN KIERAN

SOPHIE LODGE

THE UNIVERSITY FOR IDLERS

Raffaella Malaguti discovers a slothful education programme flourishing in the mountains of Campania

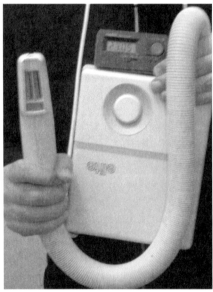

INUTILITOMETRO

In southern Italy, idling is a cherished skill that has been refined through the centuries by people like Pietrantonio Arminio who spent months trying to invent a perpetual motion machine.

In the early 1970s, he and a friend moved into a farmhouse outside their sleepy mountain village of Bisaccia, lived in true hippie style and worked full time on their ambitious project.

Now Arminio has given up on his romantic quest. He has become a sculpter and lives in Rome. But his perpetual-motion adventures have inspired a new generation of local loafers to devise Bisaccia's second potential contribution to humanity: the Università degli Accidiosi (University for Idlers).

The idea, born two years ago on a bench in Bisaccia's main square, was actually turned into a concrete project in the summer of 2003, only a year after the bench illumination. Devised and run by a group of thirtysomething former Bisaccia inhabitants the university is little more than a website for e-learning (www.unibis.org) where aspiring and real idlers can exchange knowledge on how to refine their art.

"We have all left the village but every summer we go back and we always do the same thing: nothing. We sit on a bench in the main square and loaf," explains the University's placid dean Pasquale di Donato over a plate of pasta.

"But one night some girls were there and our friend Renato wanted to impress them with a joke. He said he had a degree in distraction sciences. So we thought, 'hey, a university like that would be useful'. That's how the idea was born in practice. But the tradition was already there." Loafing is popular in Bisaccia and idling traditions run deep, as the attempt to invent the perpetual motion machine show. "There are several people who have never worked in their life; they are a hundred years old and look very well. So you ask yourself, who is better off?" continues di Donato.

Bisaccia perches on the mountains of the Campania region, in one of Italy's poorest and most remote areas. Not

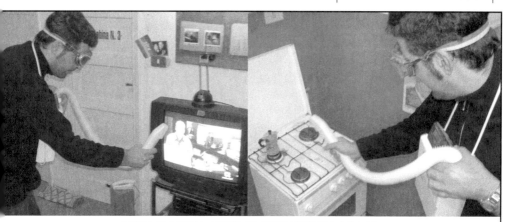

DAVIDE MASTRULLO DURING AN INUTILITOMETRO SESSION

much happens in this village which has a mere 5,000 inhabitants. And yet, it has produced several artists and all the professors of the University.

This flourishing of creative minds must be due to Bisaccia's vocation for idling. Or maybe it is because its population speaks a dialect featuring words like *speranzone*, which literally means hopeful but actually refers to someone who hopes that things –most of all work–don't happen to him. The *speranzone's* typical answer to someone asking: "what are you doing?" is, with a shrug, "what can you do?".

This concept has inspired one of first courses to be devised at the University: "Phenomenology of The Speranzone".

The other courses are "Elements of Distracted Songwriting", "Anthropology of Distraction", "Phenomenology of Free Time", "Non-useful Sciences", "Theory and Technical Elements of Walking Aimlessly", "Ergonomics of the Bench" and "Ethics of Incantation".

One of the very few essays turned in by students was submitted for "Machines and Prototypes to Save Energy". It was written by an inhabitant of Bisaccia and shows how a washing machine's engine can be used to make *passata*, the smooth tomato sauce that many southern Italians still make at home at the end of the summer. As you can imagine, passing lots of tomatoes through a vegetable mill is hard work and finding a way to avoid it is top priority for an idler.

The University's teaching methods are quite simple. Students register on the website, choose their subjects and get credits when they turn in any, excuse the word, "work". The professors suggest literature to read and post contributions. Obviously, no official degree can be obtained.

Some 90 people have registered so far and the new academic institution has caught the attention of one Italy's most productive crosswords writers and most famous linguists who has signalled it on one of his weekly columns.

As habits die hard in Bisaccia, just a couple of the 30 inhabitants who have enrolled have turned in any work so far. But some faculty members are devising a new tool: the inutilitometro (uselessness metre), aimed at measuring the degree of uselessness of a certain person in a room or in relation to an object. It is a mystery whether and how this instrument is supposed to work, but it would be useful indeed. ☕

CRAP HOLIDAYS

Will Hogan nearly gets shot while touring the Middle East

ISRAEL AND EGYPT

Foolishly keen to sample the aquatic delights of diving in Egypt and the salubrious properties of Israel's Dead Sea, my two friends and I packed our trunks and headed out to Stanstead airport where our Crap Holiday began.

Anyone who's ventured onto an El Al Israeli chartered plane to check their baggage in will promptly realise that the interrogation techniques used by their stentorian employees are the verbal equivalent of being slapped across the face by a leather glove. This savage parlez went on for about forty-five minutes. They couldn't seem to fathom why we were simply three blokes "on holiday" without any sinister reason.

Four hours after the barbarous introduction and the requisite Gin and Tonic saturated flight we touched down in Tel Aviv to more people prodding us with rifles and asking us more tricky questions.

After smoking a bit of pot with ex-pat Kibbutz escapees and attempting to charm the military girls of Tel Aviv (which simply resulted in humiliation as we simply weren't hard enough to strip an AK47 blindfolded) we lost no time in driving in a shagged hire car with Israeli number plates right into Jericho in the mistaken belief that we were on our way to the Dead Sea.

Owing to certain political forces, driving an Israeli car around there is like having a

SHOPPING MAUL

fucking great billboard permanently suspended above your head with the words "Please Attack" stencilled in meter high letters.

After numerous pedestrian shouts which roughly translated as "I kill you!" and Arab residents hurling large rocks (I kid you not) we made it in the end to the dead sea, where we floated for the next three hours. We then realised that the maximum time one should spend in the Dead Sea is under forty-five minutes. This resulted in our extremely dry skin peeling off in kebab like chunks in the mid-July sun. Driving our frazzled hides to the border of Egypt, we deposited the hire car and trundled over the border to find more people wielding guns.

Taking a taxi which looked like it was constructed from several deceased vans, ex-school trip coaches and an Austin Maestro we arrived in Dahab. We then booked into a hotel – or at least part of a hotel. The hotel hallway tapered off to a sheer drop albeit tiled right up until the massive crevice. The shower had electric cables poking tendril like out of the wall which added to the excitement of being doused in lukewarm sea water.

I promptly developed chronic diarrhoea by mid-afternoon. So bad were the anal emissions that I had to stay in the baking hotel room for the next two days occasionally flame throwing passing cockroaches with deodorant and a lighter for entertainment. As for pulling a passing traveller, this was somewhat hindered by losing my remaining contact lenses and not being to see nor dive. The latter may not sound too much of a hindrance but when one is competing to gain the affections of female travellers against hardened divers who bludge on about wrestling a ten foot sea snake to the ocean floor, then it's a problem. I stayed marooned on the beach side cafes staring into the middle distance occasionally breaking wind and constantly being "playfully" hassled by 15 pre-pubescent Bedouin girls, goading me to buy bracelets and gamble on a game of backgammon, which inevitable ended in me loosing a large quantity of shekels and having my sunglasses pinched.

The highlight had to be some show off attempting to impress some girls in the neighbouring room by climbing a palm tree (which I might add simply ran right through the three floors of the hotel) and then getting stuck on the upward facing layers of spiky bark. After much laughter and prodding we realised the prongs of bark had actually pierced his clothes and skin and thus it took about fifteen minutes for us to disengage the hapless moron. ◉

WERE HAVING A TWAT-IN! ITS LIKE A LOVE-IN! BUT WITH A FEW TWATS!

BRING A FUCKING BOTTLE!

GWYN

CRAP JOBS

Rachel Manasseh gets wired

QUALITY CONTROL TESTER

I once spent a summer in a windowless box room testing wires. The wires were attached to a handset, which was attached to a chair. My job was to see how many times I could take out and replace the handset before the wire broke. Without sabotage. The answer was usually about 10,000.

Not that it mattered; the machine that recorded the results of this task of almost unbelievable tedium was usually broken. Although this made any attempt to test the wires pointless, and in fact counterproductive, we had to continue to pretend to work anyway. The reason for this was a purely sadistic attempt to destroy our morale.

This hell hole would be trying even for a person with an unusually high boredom threshold, but the part of the job that made it a living hell was the presence of my only colleague, a foul tempered, racist old woman, who insisted on forced conversation for duration of the nine-hour day. Rather than being allowed to drift in and out of the near-death coma which nature demanded, I was instead forced

"BY THE END OF FIVE WEEKS I WAS A HUMAN WRECK"

to listen to a stream of thinly veiled insults towards minority groups, interspersed with an ongoing and highly detailed account of her dog's "battle with cancer". Occasionally, this monologue would be interrupted by a visit from an obese buffoon, who would engage my colleague in predictably unpleasant discussions on the issues of the day. In order to further destroy my faith in humanity, the radio was kept on Radio Two, at a volume slightly too high for comfort. The horrible racist old woman was a particular fan of phone-in programmes and Terry Wogan.

By the end of five weeks of employment I was a human wreck, convinced I was going blind and unable to function in normal society. The advantage of this living nightmare has been that none of my subsequent shitty jobs has seemed so bad in comparison. The disadvantage is that I have seen the darkness of the human soul. ✆

Neville by Tony Husband

THE IDLER QUESTIONNAIRE:
NICK BROOMFIELD

What time do you get up?

7.30 am

Do you leap up or lie slumbering?

Leap up

Do you smoke and drink, and if so, how much?

I don't smoke, I drink a little

How many hours work do you put in on an average day?

Around eight

Do you take holidays?

Yes, lots of them

Where do you live?

All over the place

Where do you work?

All over the place

Where do you think?

All over the place

What are your three greatest pleasures?

Sex, travelling and food

Do you like money?

Not particularly

Are you happy?

Yes

How many hours do you sleep at night/day?

About six

What are you reading at the moment?

Wild Swans by Yung Chang

If it came to the crunch, would you choose money or art?

Art

What have you been thinking about?

About the need to procreate one's species

Who are your heroes?

Lord Byron, Erroll Flynn and Bertrand Russell

Any advice for young people?

Keep your boots clean, your bowels open and don't piss against the wind

Do you like to go a-wandering?

Yes, very much

What is paradise?

Seeing Tony Blair slipping on a banana skin 🍵

GRAP TOWNS USA

CHARLOTTE, N. CAROLINA

Population: 54.000 **Unemployment:** 6.3% **Famous residents:** Stephen Davies (NFL)

Charlotte is a city without a soul. The "Downtown" area consists entirely of gross, morally-bereft, capitalist towers. There are no stores, no pharmacies, nothing except expensive bars that hoover up the vast wealth of the blinkered Prada-draped drones that shuffle around its bland, corporate edifice. 🍵

THANKS TO ELEANOR EVANS

PETER'S PIECES

Two pieces of lovely weirdness from
the keyboard of Peter Doherty

BEING LEGS

Unsubstantiated hype: being heavy, rotten, artificial legs. Legs we most of us take for granted. Envied by cripples. Two people mocking the afflicted, mocking each other, these close friends, hurtful with agility (demanded), skill (jammy git), violence (psycho, all in all), patience (guilt), and malice (unfriendly advice).

Reading eyes (older lady in the corner, forgotten old dear, lost in a blank, stiff, headache life). Yes gin dear.

Anagram enigma, possibly genius prose. Mind you, that was the sarcastic offering of critic's shittermen, lifeless reviews, chickless headens.

Up the top of the first page of the three like a kipper in the mush, mush pinpointed the suburban Harrow canal path to the very long ragged swarm of wires, rupturing the berry and plum trees dangling on for dear life to the steepening banks of shite that walled our watery industrial veins, that is to say like spindly pink arteries busy with billions of such and such, barging their way into modern lifeflow; exactly like the riverless trenches of the desert shores all in African places, only dry. Gulp.

Artless poseur that he was, canny cunning Jal, the obedient servant of squalid abnormal impulses, sort senseless remedies for nv s ble barriers in the body and bloody brain. Bilo typer for two seconds into it, no cunt knows what a I men hisself... you blink slowly and reveal in technicolour, our *déjà vu* me, your old friend, and trusted, or someone admiration or spite and shite spot on, tut-tutting and "oh my God, it's terrible" remarks that's come out of my mouth if you asked me how a I me and that self all in my head and everywhere you'd care to give or take a flywheeel... and flywheel fuck, or fig, or fucking fig, Costa Rice/Scottish and Cameroon and Gazza in Italia 90.

Bilo indeed, sport Billy too. In awe of Chris Waddle and histories of Marsh, Bowles, Wegerle... when he beat ten men, all nutmegs. Bamboozles and shimmies up the shorts and down the bum's steep angled pillars. Being legs, you get me bro, coz when I flow, I'm off to obliterate the sodding pain and horror of my lifecore.

LOOPBILO

"I like the fact," he says... images of decay... then: "Sorry, Pete. Can I pinch another rolly?"

"Yeah."

Typing, I hear other voices.

"Send a cab, there and back."

"Sorry, yeah, from there to Hackney and back, yeah. I haven't used this phone

for weeks, no, weeks. Yeah, thank you."

"Strange," he says, the other fella.

"Bring a tenner back."

"No, we need a tenner for the cab."

Low, rumbling tape replays of the everynight's noise: voices, sparks and sweet-forming music. All along the night, we patter, voices clatter chicken, steal guitars, smoke sweet perfume.

"You on the Internet, Pete?"

"Na, you're joking, aren't you?" This pad-clunk keyboard was born with its square-headed desk for neckle, pal, long before the bands were broadening.

Ticking and clocking without the lightly morning that caught me surprisingly far, there medium-sized light giant beanstalks still grow where I scattered the seeds last summer and a liberty lad is in these times of unlocked doors apt to outdoors with birdsong and adventure. Shall we... 🐌

PETE LOVEDAY

BILL & ZED'S BAD ADVICE

WE'VE FUCKED UP OUR LIVES. NOW IT'S YOUR TURN

Dear Zen Masters,

I recently compiled a series of books, *Rubbish Places* and *Rubbish Ways to Earn a Living*. Imagine my surprise, then, when the BBC published a book called *Rubbish Motors*. My lawyer said it looks like my books and feels like my books. He thinks we have some sort of case. What course of action would you recommend?

Jim Rubbish

Zed: First things first, Mr Rubbish, sir. Of course your filthy lawyer bastard will think you have a case. If you buggered the queen and set fire to her corgis the squirming little soiled underpant bastard would somehow work out a way of justifying your actions, that's their job. They compete at seeing who is the best liar, it's a highly lucrative game, bamboozling idiots like yourself in a highly technical jargon specifically designed to keep you in the dark.

Mr Rubbish, my simple advice is to take it in a generous fashion, imitation being the sincerest form of flattery and all that.
Bill: My advice may be coming to you a bit late in life, but here it is anyway: never lose sight of the ideals you had as a young man. Do not let those ideals be clouded by your baser ambitions. The obvious impetus behind this recently compiled series of books, you mentioned, was not born from the ideals of your youth but from those baser ambitions.

You were obviously tempted by the quick buck, with these tawdry, impulse-buy, stocking-fillers. Being a man of letters you should be employing your wit and wisdom to produce work that will ennoble the nation.

Dear Zen Masters,

Me and my ancestors have been bored since 1760. Do you have any advice?

W. Morris, Epping Forest

Zed: The question in reality, young Master Morris, dear boy, is in fact, are you really bored, or are you, in fact, boring?
Bill: Well, William, I was wondering when you would rear your ugly head again. If you had only known how your dreadful wallpaper patterns have bored the nation since you first started churning them out back when Dickens was first learning to sharpen his pencil. My advice to you is to commandeer the good Doctor's Tardis, get back to the 1860s. Once there, burn all your sketchbooks before they make it to the printing presses and use your artistic bent to invent modernism before all those French and Irish do.

Dear Zen Masters,

I am feeling guilty because I didn't give anything to the Tsunami appeal. No cash, no clothes, no blankets, nothing. Any advice on dealing with the guilt?
G. Debord, Leeds

Zed: I know what you mean, all those poor child prostitutes put out of work, Gary Glitter and all his friends leaving the area in droves. A human tragedy. Bill and I are organizing a field trip out their early next month to make sure they get back to work as soon as possible, please feel free to join us.

Bill: Tsunami! Tsunami! Tsunami! Who the fuck had heard of this word, let alone knew how to spell it before last Christmas and now it's a bleedin' fashion accessory. I feel sorry for all those starving Africans that nobody gives a shit about now.

Dear Zen Masters,

I recently bought five bantam chickens. At first, they were quite good in that they laid eggs every day. Then they started to disappear. Now there is just one left, and I don't know where it lays its eggs, if any. Do you think I should stick with bantams or go for a regular breed?
F. Giles

Zed: Why don't you just go down to fucking Tesco's like the bleeding rest of us, you free range fucking idiot?
Bill: Ignore Z's advice, at times he's just a cynical townie. Don't shop at Tesco's, what ever you do, it's just more money going to prop up the Zionist fantasy of a land flowing with milk and honey, when we can all see it is just a scrap of desert. What was the subject again? Chickens, that was it. I live in the country. I keep chickens. I know about these sorts of things. Keep buying chickens, but not fuckin' Bantams. Get yourself some Hisex, they don't look pretty, they are tough old birds and they are good layers. As for Mr Fox, you have to let him have his cut. Now that hunting has been banned his cut might get a bit bigger.

Dear Zen Masters,

What time of year do you recommend manuring your garden? And do you favour regular household compost, cow muck or horse muck?
W. Cobbett

Zed: I try to stay away from all forms of shit as much as possible, especially if it means smearing it all over the stuff that I eat. I tell you, mate, there's something fucking wrong with you, there fucking is. Putting fucking shit on your fucking spuds? Jesus fucking Christ, we don't live in fucking India you know. I hope you wash your hands before you start having a go on your missus. Blimey, the poor girl.
Bill: Horseshit for roses, cowshit for cabbages and for the rest you can't better human shit. Ban you and your family from using the indoor lav and get them down the vegetable plot pissing and shitting in rotation. As for having a go on the missus, the muckier it is the more she will like it.

CONVERSATIONS

RAOUL VANEIGEM

Laurence Rémila meets the great philosopher and writer, one of the prime movers in the Paris riots of 1968, now living quietly in Belgium

H e's been dragging round the reputation of being one of the lynchpins of the *International Situationiste* for over thirty years. Raoul Vaneigem's *Traité de savoir-vivre à l'usage des jeunes générations*, (*The Revolution of Everyday Life*) was published the same year (1967) as his *compagnon de route* Guy Debord's *La Société du Spectacle*. It was one of the texts that anticipated – sparked off, if you like – the May 1968 revolts, its discourse inspiring the *Enragés* of Nanterre, its words ending up on countless walls.

And when giddy 1968 gave way to dazed 1969, he was out (after eight years of activisim), leaving the *IS* to Debord and his excommunications. A prolific author, he's since published thirty-odd books. Where his books differ from those of other situationists is that this former philosophy student has always included personal reflections on bettering oneself. He also writes books that bear directly on their times. When France experienced massive strikes in 1995, his *Avertissement aux écoliers et aux lycéens*, addressed to the striking students, was a must-have.

Today, at 71 years old, Vaneigem is as radical as ever. He lives in the Belgian countryside, refuses public appearances and face-to-face interviews (he will only answer in writing) and does what he's always done: write for anyone who questions the way they're encouraged to live their life. Here's a piece of advice for you, dear English-speaking reader: get hold of his recent *Modestes propositions aux grévistes: Pour en finir avec ceux qui nous empêchent de vivre en escroquant le bien public* (Verticales, 2004) – a fierce defence of our right to rip off the State – and get that cute French thing working at the tube-station deli to translate bits of it for you. Just make sure to fare-dodge when you go.

IDLER: Can one live without working?

VANEIGEM: We can only live without working. We only work through necessity, to survive. Life starts when one stops working. Work is incompatible with life which is essentially creative. Life is a permanent invention, survival is nothing but a monotonous work of reproduction.

IDLER: What do you think of the success of Corrine Maier's book, *Bonjour Paresse* (or even the work of the *Idler*, which has done a lot to promote the idea of the benefits of idleness)? Is it a more accessible way of approaching issues that concern you? Or simply a way of ignoring them?

VANEIGEM: Yesterday, capitalism accorded the worker the leisure of recuperating a little of his strength of production so's to be able to go back to the factory and give the best of his energy. Today, when the modern worker is freed from work-hours during which he has enriched the ruling classes, he continues to increase the profits of the capital by spending his salary and by becoming a slave in the supermarkets. Leisure has become a work of consumption.

The advantage of idleness, is that it is not – unlike leisure – the ally of work. It doesn't integrate the rhythm of labour, it is part of the rhythm of life. It is through it that creativity ripens, that we get to know ourselves, our desires. When we leave it – because prolonging it soon turns to boredom – it doesn't incite us to throw ourselves in the frenzy of work but rather to discover the pleasures of creating and the art of creating pleasures for ourselves. One cannot live without idleness and one cannot live through idleness (apart from making others work for us, which turns the pleasure into ignominy). Idleness and creation are inseparable, it is a good thing to remind ourselves of that as only creativity can rid us of work, as there is only imaginative ingenuity to subvert oppression.

IDLER: You sometimes say you've been writing the same book for forty years. As you do so, do you consciously try to make it more practical? And how does the start of this project, written forty-odd years ago, fit in with what you've written more recently?

VANEIGEM: Every book is the product of its time as well as of an individual. Radicality consists in seizing beings and things at the root, which is life. My radicality hasn't changed. It becomes more precise as changes in the dominant world show how merchant totalitarianism progresses and how it produces, in the heart of its evolution, that which denies it.

May 1968 sparked off a change in society that most people still feel confusedly today, though they are unable to formulate it, such is the force of the inertia keeping our modes of thinking locked into the prejudices of the past. One day though, we'll have to admit that May 1968 marked a complete break with the majority of patriarchal values that had, for several millennia, governed collective and individual ways of behaviour, all kept under the thumb of religious institutions, ideologies, the army, the police, hierarchised power, paternal and marital authority. Situationist ideas propagated the refusal of work and sacrifice, the denunciation of ideologies, the rejection of all authority, by opposing the primacy of life to survival, and by underlining the growing importance accorded to nature, to woman, to child, to creation, to desire. It is this consciousness that I spend my time trying to reignite. However, this consciousness, which could result simply from a voluntarist attitude, meets today – with the crisis caused by the mutation of capitalism - the objective conditions that comfort it. What else have we seen?

We have witnessed, since the consumerism of the 1960s, the accelerated development of a financial capitalism that, instead of re-dynamising production by using a part of the profits, now only buys stock to speculate. Confined to short-term profitability, imprisoned in a financial bubble condemned to implode, this sclerosed capitalism will give way, sooner or later, to a neo-capitalism that will discover, in energies that are free and renewable, a new mode of production and a source of profits that manages to avoid the threat weighing on petrol supplies and on nuclear power stations, both of which are increasingly contested. The emergence of a new re-natured agriculture and a technological "alternative", which prefers to ally itself to nature rather than to pillage it, allows us to conjecture a possible going beyond this merchant civilisation and the beginning of a humane society.

But such is the omnipresence of the spectacle – which considers that what it doesn't recognise doesn't exist, that we only see the immensity of the Titanic without realising its hold has burst. Almost all of our field of vision is monopolised by the triumph of merchant totalitarianism, resignation and servility, the nihilism of speculators, of fetishism and money, of fear and self-censorship.

The old capitalism founded on the pillage of natural resources and on financial accumulation in a closed-circuit will soon be shipwrecked. A new capitalism is here, which is supplanting it, and which we will have to fight because, under cover of privileging the quality of products, non-polluting energies, the primacy of the worth of usage and humanist values, it has no other aim but to perpetuate the reign of all that's mercantile. To limit oneself to vituperating the sclerosed shape, taken over by small-time speculators, while ignoring the new "ecological" capitalism in development – with the firm intention of

The advantage of idleness, is that it is not – unlike leisure – the ally of work

I don't suppose that my desires are those of each and every person; I simply think that many people are animated by a similar will for living

liquidating it too – it is to claim to destroy what is destroying itself and destroying oneself at the same time. It is to resign oneself, with cries of revolt and indignation, to sinking with the ship. For me it's a particularly morbid form of revolutionary imposture.

IDLER: Is it important for you to address your works to high-school kids, to strikers, to well-defined groups of readers, as you have done with your recent works?

VANEIGEM: I'm the first person I address myself to. I try to disentangle the problems I find myself faced with each day and to solve them by integrating them in a global project of transformation of the world. I've made my longing for a life unceasingly more passionate the motor of a radical subversion. I don't suppose that my desires are those of each and every person; I simply think that many people are animated by a similar will for living and that, as a consequence, certain readers find in my texts an echo of their own preoccupations. It is neither the number of readers – nor their status – that interests me, it is the interest they take in my way of acting through picking up what they deem useful in my books and by discarding the rest. As for the accountancy of the passing years, it is time to do justice by recalling that if survival has an age, life is ageless.

IDLER: You've lived in the Belgian countryside for many years. Do you feel cut off from the outside world? How do you act to be in touch with the problems of those to whom your books are explicitly addressed?

VANEIGEM: Everyday life is the only real territory that's ours to try and liberate. The fight for emancipation is an imposture when it strays from that territory and falls into intellectuality, militancy, thought separated from life, ideology. The questions people ask themselves about an existence from which real life is far too often absent are fundamentally the same the world over. The trouble is that they think they're solving their existential problems by cutting themselves off from them, by accepting bits of

nonsense that populist and cronyist politics sell them unceasingly through the news and in media clichés. Where is the fighting spirit? With those who go out into the streets and shout slogans and then go home to relapse the following day into the same ruts? With the *casseurs* (breakers) who let off steam by defending the right to destroy in a society that already destroys everything including itself? With the socialist, Trotskyite, ex-communist, libertarian dinosaurs for whom the world hasn't changed any more than their sclerosed way of thinking? These people exist only by proxy, they accept to be nothing in a world that annihilates them. What's missing the most today, is the consciousness of both our creative richness and the possibility we have of creating situations that free us from our oppressions: the quest for survival-money, the need to work, the boredom produced by the spectacle of the living eviscerated, the falsification of desires, the frustration leading to hatred, the cycle of repression and release, the weight of archaisms. I think that my aspiration for a radical change has some chance of meeting a certain number of individual resolutions which, through their specificity, go in the same direction. I'm certain that life always triumphs over the negation of life.

In the absence of a conscience that's attentive to the will to live and to the mutations and social changes taking place, all there is is admissions of failure. Never have the conditions for setting the basis for a humane society been so favourable and never have inertia, passivity, resignation, voluntary servitude and impotency triumphed so. The social struggles have given way to political populism and to corrupt face-offs in which the religious and nationalist old-timers lend their patched-up banners. Giving up is what many militants do best, who have never ceased to brandish them to salute just about any cause, apart from those that involve building their own lives.

The social struggle has to re-invent itself. It should reject the archaisms that imprison it – political populism, bureaucratic trade-unionism, militancy, ideologies – and base itself on the conscience and individuals' desire for life.

IDLER: Is it important to confront the fruit of your readings to the life of all?

VANEIGEM: What is important is that each person draws his knowledge from his personal experience and if a book or a speech can enlighten him, help him to live better or to eradicate that which is stopping him from living better, all the better.

IDLER: In 1960/61, you discovered the strikes in Belgium, and it is a question which you regularly come back to. What's changed since the start of the sixties with regards to this?

VANEIGEM: All reasons are good for stopping to work but that isn't enough if we want to obtain more than the crumbs that your employers deign to throw you. Most of the major strikes from the past were about protest. They'd paralyse the system of capitalistic exploitation and exert pressure on it. They'd last the time needed for him to make a few concessions and satisfy a part of the workers' demands, these demands managed not by themselves but alas by trade-unionist *bureaucraties*. In exchange, the employers would obtain that they go back to work and it is of course from the exploitation of the work that they draw their profit, their plus-value. As for the trade-unions, shouting victory, they'd consolidate their hold on the proletariat.

The old idea of a general strike that would overthrow capitalism and lead to a revolution has never been proposed with either conviction or pertinence. The communist ideology, this imposture bureaucratized by Leninism, claimed to regulate the revolutionary conscience for decades. We'll long remember the programmatic formula of the Stalinist Maurice Thorez: "One has to know how to end a strike." The point is, strikes were never revolutionary at a period where they could have been. Of course, they have improved the level of survival for the masses. But as beneficial as they were for the workers, the relative well-being it gave them would end up profiting capitalism itself which, from the years 1955-1960 on, started to draw the majority of its profits from the consumer sector rather than from production. Salary increases are directly recovered by the dominant system thanks to the proliferation of supermarkets. Slowly but surely, consumerism has devoured everything, including class consciousness. We've seen a market democracy be propagated on the model of big retail stores where each person has the freedom to choose a huge variety of products on condition he pays for them before leaving. The primary objective is to incite the consumer to buy just about anything just so long as the volume of purchases increases, the utility and quality of the products have decreased while the artifices of seduction aimed at customers, the techniques of promotion, that's to say the promotion of the useless and the parasitic, have unceasingly gained in importance. Information is nothing but advertising.

We are now prey to a populist system that governs politics and business indifferently, as well as corporatist demands, religions and ideologies. There is a single demand capable of smashing this system that destroys all the vital sectors of society, it is the right to live, the right to create a milieu that facilitates and favours an existence that's truly humane. What I recommend are strikes demanding gratuity. Gratuity is absolutely antithetic to market economy, it is both a practical way of combat and a way of thinking that's in accord with this generosity of the alive that manifests itself in the feelings of love, friendship, solidarity or the pleasure of giving. It is this conscience of gratuity perfectly applicable in the primary sector that has to be propagated everywhere and stimulate invention. Have the trains, the metros, the buses running freely and you will provoke healthy emulation everywhere, you will awaken the creativity of each person.

The market for renewable energies is the driving force of this new capitalism that is emerging little by little and opposing its dynamism to the capitalism which, though still dominant, is sinking in stock speculation and is threatened by the rarefaction of fossil energies. However, even though they are seen as a source of profit, alternative energies currently in development implicate a principle of gratuity which it's up to us to brandish as a weapon against the new masters, whose exploitation is readying itself to take over from the one we knew before.

Raoul Vaneigem's latest book is *A Declaration of Human Rights: On the Sovereignty of Life as Surpassing the Rights of Man*, Liz Heron (Translator), Pluto Press Ltd. His *Revolution Of Everyday Life* is available from Rebel Press

FEATURES

GROW UP

Actor and comic Keith Allen presents the
A-Z of his life so far, with cock-out elan

"**H**e will either win the Victoria Cross or go to prison." So said Keith Allen's
headmaster, back in 1966. As a young man he was so angry that he ended
up fighting a one-man war. Against himself. Since then, he's been
renowned for his extrovert and contentious behaviour, his radical opinions
and his acting pedigree. This is Keith's A-Z of life as he knows it. He tackles
everything from acting to crack waxes, euthanasia to naked air travel.
Plus we feature a still from Keith's Naked 2005 Calendar.

A **IS FOR ACTING:** I could have been a footballer if my criminal career hadn't got in the way. Age sixteen I was due to have trials at Southampton and Leeds United when I was arrested for nicking a wallet from the locker room of a local Sunday league team. I was never criminally minded but I was a little fucking thief from time to time. Opportunistic crime. My old man was pleased that I got sent to borstal. As a submariner and a strict disciplinarian, he hoped that it would get me on the straight and narrow. Instead I spent long afternoons scrubbing the canteen floor with Tony Diskin and we would put on voices and play games. I learnt how to make people laugh. I took my O-levels in borstal too after it was presented to me that I could become a student – of what I didn't care; being called a student was a step up from being a thief, plus I got paid for it. I don't think that this was the kind of straight and narrow my old man had in mind for me. Mincing about on stage was not how he saw his son. But I didn't start out with a great urge to be an actor; I did it because it made women look at me in a different way. David Williams was my mentor. Because of him I took part in the gang show and did sketches.

I joined Swansea Little Theatre with a view to fucking other men's wives. Which I did. It seemed to me that the only reason to go on to study at drama college was to fuck girls. Which of course I did. But even after enrolling at the Welsh College of Music and Drama, I was no nearer to discovering what it was to be an actor because I was too busy skipping classes to play football. The theory of acting – the "living in the truthfulness of the moment" – was a small dot on the horizon.

Most of us are beholden to other

I joined Swansea Little Theatre with a view to fucking other men's wives. Which I did.

people's expectations. But other people's expectations didn't exist for me – so long as I was happy, that was all that mattered. This gave me a wonderful advantage over other people my age because, unfettered by conscience, I did exactly what I wanted.

B IS FOR BOLLOCKS: "Bollocks for Boats" is my appeal for cash to help buy boats for victims of the Asian tsunami, flaunting my nakedness in the form of a calendar for 2005. It seemed like a good idea at the time. Until the day of the shoot. The speed with which the wave hit the shore was proportional to the speed with which my cock retreated in to my belly button. There have been a few remarks made about plastic surgery but I know the truth and so do the thousands of women victims skewered by my manhood; it was a cold day.

Returning to the calendar, it went down so well with my close friends that an exclusive limited edition print run of 30 was woefully inadequate. Suddenly people were hearing about it in LA. Kate Moss offered me £500 in the Groucho Club for one. I refused, saying there were only enough for close friends and she replied that I owed her mother an apology and so could I send her one? I immediately rang my dear friend and society photographer Tiggy Wiggy Kennedy, the woman responsible for capturing all of the man you see before

We'll sell pictures of your hairy bottom issuing forth daffodils for fifty quid a pop

you. She echoed my sentiments – saying she was swamped by demand for said articles of my article. She asked me if I would agree to another print run that we could sell to raise cash for her friend who is on the front line in Sri Lanka helping fishermen get their lives back together.

"What?" I replied facetiously. "My bollocks for some boats?"

"Yes Keith, we'll sell pictures of your hairy bottom issuing forth daffodils for fifty quid a pop."

"Oh brilliant," I replied gleefully. "Forty nine quid for me and a quid for the fishermen." Sounds about fucking right.

"No Keith," said Tiggy, unamused by my distasteful bravura. "You get nothing except the satisfaction of putting something back."

As I strode purposefully towards The Groucho, I suddenly realised that the fact that my my testicles would remove the big bollock that is Geldof from the front page of charity fundraising was all the moral justification I needed.

B IS FOR BACK, SACK AND CRACK: I'm a hairy actor. That's true. And I don't wear any underpants. But what is the point of having some gay male nurse ask you to hold your bollocks to one side while he proceeds to touch your arsehole with a waxy strip and then pull so hard you lose your eyebrows in the nuclear

blast of pain? I prefer the "Hole, Mole and Dole" – where your girlfriend trims your nose, your hairy moles and then picks up your social security cheque. Less pain more gain.

I've noticed that footballers, once the archetypal man's man, have started favouring the hairless look preferred by gay men. One can only assume that Messrs. Lampard and Beckham have moved not to Chelsea or Madrid but to the village people.

Once a man bit my cock in a fight. I had to have it stitched at St Mary's Paddington.

B IS FOR BERNARD MATTHEWS: Creator of battery farming.

B IS FOR BOB GELDOF: See under C for Cunt.

B IS FOR BRITISH PUBLIC

C IS FOR CAPITALISM

C IS FOR CRACK WHORES: Class knows no barrier when it comes to crack whores. The amused snorting in daddy's library bears no resemblance to the gutter-like sniffling of the bitches from Bermondsey but they are both undoubtedly crack whores. Classless but classy.

C IS FOR CUNTS: See British Public.

C IS FOR CUNT

D IS FOR DAMES: I've had the pleasure of knowing two Great Dames of the Theatre carnally. It was in the 1980s and early 1990s when I was acquiring a reputation in the theatre for being a liar and pig as well as something of an acTOR.

It was undoubtedly the offer of a large slice of rough that drew these undulating ladies to me. Who could possibly believe that these two buffoons who strutted around in ballooning kaftans and turbans sold by Hampstead Bazaar were up for being rogered senseless after paying attention to the business end of a bottle of amyl?

C IS FOR CAPTAIN: In 2001, after splitting up with my second wife, I bought a boat to live on. Maybe it's because I'm rootless or maybe it's because I'm a navy baby, but I always thought I'd end up on water. I searched the internet (or rather I got a bitch to do it, as I'm computer illiterate). The first boat advertisement I came across said: "A DIY nightmare or the beginning of a lifelong love affair." It turned out to be both. *Kaapsedraii* is a 1901 one-hundred-and-ten-foot Dutch barge. It was commandeered by the Nazis to transport ammunition through the Dutch canals. Now it was my home. I took ownership in Rotterdam and realised that this rusting hulk of a ship had an interior like the chest cavity of a rotting antelope. I employed a boat builder to start the epic journey needed to turn this cadaverous

beast into a star feature in *Houseboat Interiors* magazine. He met me in Rotterdam with a bag of rusty tools and a rather idiotic West Country gaze, but I tried not to let that put me off. I was so excited to own a boat. After years of pretending to enjoy cohabiting with wives I was finally off on a maiden voyage into my future. The plan was to start the work en route as we sailed her home to London. What followed was a voyage through the bowels of hell.

Every captain picks up a crew. A legion of men who are prepared to follow you wherever you go. I only had Pockets, a cook who claims to have once cleaned Joan Collins' shoes. Along with Arthur, the village idiot builder, we recruited Roy from Amsterdam and Pablo, one of the world's leading percussionists. All of whom had the same

knowledge of marine navigation as a packet of crisps.

We suddenly found ourselves the meat in the sandwich of two of the world's largest supertankers, having strayed into the shipping lane of the Zuider Zee. Having lost power, the vessel was pitching and rolling and threatening to turn over. Had she have done so, that would have been it. Being flat-bottomed, *Kaapsedraai* would have sunk like a stone. My witless crew, apart from my able seaman pilot Tom, was oblivious, slewing around below in a pond of gin. Practically everything that wasn't tethered down was thrown about; Roy was nearly killed by a flying washing machine. Quite why I had bought a washing machine before I had anything to plug it into is another part of me that comes under W for "What women will never understand".

F IS FOR FULHAM

M IS FOR MACKEREL: A wonderful fish. If ever there was a fish glad to be just a face in the crowd, it's the mackerel. Never to be seen in a glass case in a poxy pub, this fucker swims and dies. In fact, I would go as far as to say, If I was to be a fish, it would be the mackerel. Can a mackerel be an individual? I think not, but this is not to limit its status as the embodiment of the power of the masses.

N IS FOR NAKED AIR TRAVEL

N IS NARCOTICS ANONYMOUS

N IS FOR NIGHTCLUBS: I've run two of them in my life. The first was in Val d'Isère when I met Steve Barron, the film director and owner of Limelight nightclub. Set up in my hotel room while promoting *The Yob* at a film festival. I took the beds out of my hotel room and set up a ghetto blaster. We bought beer from the supermarket and sold it at a pound a bottle. Suddenly there were

I've always had a hatred of overhead lighting since my days in Pentonville Prison

queues down to the street and film people all heard about this new night spot. Because ski resorts don't do impromptu. Everything about snow says "planning". Think about it. When have you ever seen a hippy, a market stall or a poor person in a ski resort? I've decided that snow is the most conservative environment.

The other nightclub I ran was called Beautiful Contradictions in the heart of the West End. Some Arabs owned the gaff and put their heavies on the door. It nearly destroyed the cred of the club as they turned Galliano away for wearing Galliano trainers. Hang on a minute, I've suddenly realised that I actually hate nightclubs – because I just don't see the point. They are all about sex. Nothing wrong with that apart from its vulgarity. I am no stranger to vulgarity but I have always preferred to be the only person being vulgar. A dancefloor full of panting, sexually-charged young people makes me feel squeamish. Urgh.

O IS FOR ON THE RUN

P IS FOR PANTYLINER: A song I made up with my kids.

P IS FOR PETS: Bitches – that is, girl dogs – seem to like me. They want to lick me to death. It really is incredible, the effect I have on them. Do I exude some kind of inner warmth? They say that people who appear to be nice are often cunts – well it works that people

BUY IDLER T-SHIRTS

It may have taken us ten years, but we've finally come up with some new designs

WORK KILLS

LAZINESS IS NOT A CRIME

Lady of leisure

BACK

BACK

BACK

FRONT

FRONT

FRONT

Still ONLY £20

idle

idle

BACK

BACK

FRONT

FRONT

who appear to be cunts are actually lovely people. I think girl dogs can sense my kind heart and desire to love.

I have always had pets. As a youth, I went grape-picking in Provence with my girlfriend. We had no money and nowhere to stay. We found a rubbish tip and I built a house out of concrete breezeblocks. We adopted a pet magpie. We nearly got married because of it. Much later in my life I had a pet pig. My girlfriend at the time wouldn't let me have it in the house so it lived in the car and shat down the gearstick. I couldn't change gear without releasing the fresh stench of pig shit.

S IS FOR SQUATTING: I squatted in Eaton Square. It was here I took over a three storey house complete with a ballroom. Suddenly all my friends wanted to come and stay. I even got in the paper as "The King Of The Squatters."

T IS FOR TATTOOS: My rather limited offering to machismo is a blurred mono tattoo of a dog on my left arm. Not for me the Dionysian expanse of a lion's head but a cartoon copy of Scooby Doo (the only dog the tattooist had) that represents Rinka, Norman Scott's Great Dane. For those of you who don't remember, Norman Scott was Liberal Party leader Jeremy Thorpe's secret gay lover. After Scott threatened to expose him, Thorpe sent someone down to shoot Rinka in an attempt to keep Scott quiet. To me, Rinka symbolised the struggle between the fascist state and the freedom of the individual... dog. Poor Rinka was the only innocent in the affair. More importantly, the retelling of the story of my tattoo always guaranteed me a portion with the older married ladies, those ageing stalwarts of the liberal era who suddenly saw me as an animal-loving freedom-fighting hero. So, up

yours, lads with the big tattoos.

U IS FOR UPLIGHTING: My latest job is playing the indifferent Dr Whitman in the *Bodies* series for the BBC. Filmed in a disused mental hospital in Menston, West Yorkshire, I moved in to an executive loft apartment in a village called Baildon and discovered uplighting. I've always had a hatred of overhead lighting since my days in Pentonville Prison. Anyway. I have been told that uplighters are very 1990s. Well, Up North it's still very much on the way up. And I myself don't give a fuck because I like it.

W IS FOR WORKERS' REVOLUTIONARY PARTY: In the early 1980s I was sailing new waters looking for a portion. Politics seemed to be a good idea. I needed something radical but not too meaningful. The combination of cutting edge politics and crotchless panties was a sure-fire winner. I started to sell *News Line*, the paper of the Workers' Revolutionary Party outside lingerie shops frequented by despicably bourgeois housewives. I would get home at night used up and spat out and always with a full complement of *News Line*. If only I could have flogged the idea of freedom for the workers as energetically as I tugged at pant strings! But as a working class bloke viciously defending the freedom of the individual I found party politics flawed. It added up to the stifling of individuality, something that is at the root of my need to fight. But the fighting and protesting about oppression or poverty has always come from a sense of protecting my own freedom. I suppose everyone has their own reasons for representing a cause. Mine was myself.

Z IS FOR ZOROASTRIANISM. ⌂

TO BE CONTINUED...

A

MEMOIR

OF

ROBERT BLINCOE,

𝕬𝖓 𝕺𝖗𝖕𝖍𝖆𝖓 𝕭𝖔𝖞;

SENT FROM THE WORKHOUSE OF ST. PANCRAS, LONDON,
AT SEVEN YEARS OF AGE,

TO ENDURE THE

Horrors of a Cotton-Mill,

THROUGH HIS INFANCY AND YOUTH,

WITH A MINUTE DETAIL OF HIS SUFFERINGS,

BEING

THE FIRST MEMOIR OF THE KIND PUBLISHED.

BY JOHN BROWN.

MANCHESTER:
PRINTED FOR AND PUBLISHED BY J. DOHERTY, 37, WITHY-GROVE.
1832.

THE REAL OLIVER TWIST

Nicholas Blincoe blames his great-great-great grandfather, possibly the model for Oliver Twist, for the serfdom we suffer today

From the workhouse to our house. Like any war, the War on Work needs an enemy – a name to put to our pain. Well, I know his name: Robert Blincoe, my great-great-grandfather. Born in 1792 and abandoned at St Pancras workhouse at four, he was deemed too small and weak to become a chimney boy and so, at seven, he was sold to a mill-owner in Nottinghamshire. Robert Blincoe was a child slave, propelling the Industrial Revolution forwards. Yet for all his suffering, there is no doubting his guilt: we are in bondage today, because of that boy.

Litton Mill lay by a racing stream whose waters powered its weaving looms. Almost all the workers were children, unpaid, living on-site in dormitories. The children were woken at four am and routinely worked seventeen hours a day; rather longer than the hours stipulated by the 1802 Bill for the Protection of Infant Paupers, but few outsiders ever visited the factory in its remote valley. In any case, the magistrates and doctors who ought to have enforced the law were friends of the mill owner.

Today, Litton Mill is a complex of residential apartments. The sites of atrocities are routinely

The buying and selling of children was seen as a way of covering the Parishes' expenses

turned into museums or monuments but there are an awful lot of museums to our industrial heritage: what else can we do with all those bloody mills? Let the present inhabitants of Litton Mill enjoy their homes and sleep in peace. There is a better way of remembering my ancestor: thanks to a crusading journalist and a radical publisher, we have his life story – *A Memoir of Robert Blincoe* – a book that led to two centuries of industrial reforms.

Indentured apprenticeship is a peculiar form of slavery. Back then, the care of orphaned or abandoned children fell to the local parish; to take in a child, feed and clothe them and give them a trade, was viewed as charity. Children would be apprenticed for a set number of years: Robert Blincoe was an apprentice from the age of seven

to twenty-one. The buying and selling of children was seen as a way of covering the parishes' expenses, so a thriving slave market was justified through humbug and hypocrisy. With industrialization, all pretence that the children were apprenticed to a craft was abandoned. In Nottingham, Robert Blincoe spent his days in repetitive and dangerous work on heavy machinery. His memoirs describe a work-mate, an older girl of ten, being dragged into a machine, tossed around and finally dragged out, every bone in her body broken and her head pulped. Litton Mill had such a high mortality rate that the owners began to use two cemeteries, in parishes several miles apart, to hide the true figures. Often the children simply collapsed at their machines, at which point they were wheeled away in barrows and dumped in the sleeping quarters where they either lived or died. All the children were lice-ridden and malnourished, most deaths were due to hunger and disease. The children even ate the bone-meal that the mill-owners supplied as a scouring agent, saving money on soap for their weekly wash. Robert escaped, but was soon captured and returned for the five shilling reward, afterwards, he was chained to his machine with leg-irons. The children faced other punishments: suspended by the arms from rafters, having weights hung from their ears by clamps, and being beaten while stood in a skip, to prevent them moving.

It seems incredible to recount this now, but Robert Blincoe chose to stay on at Litton Mill after his apprenticeship ended. He felt he had nowhere else to go. Yet one year later, he was thrown out with thirty shillings in his hand and six months wages owing. The mill had no use for labourers, when they could command slaves.

A Memoir of Robert Blincoe was written in 1822 and took seven years to find a publisher – by which time the author, John Brown, had committed suicide. Once published, the *Memoir* was a hit, going through three editions between 1829 and 1832. The book is credited as a major force behind the industrial reform acts of the 1830s and as the source material for Charles Dickens' *Oliver Twist*

(1837). It is for this reason that I say my Great-great-grandfather is responsible for all the ills of modern life. To adopt the argument of French historian Michel Foucault, Robert Blincoe can be credited with the invention of both factories and children. One might retort, of course, that children and factories have always existed. But, as Foucault argued in books on the birth of the modern hospital or prison, when we speak of patients or of criminals – or, here, of factory-workers and children – the meaning of these groups is determined by the institutions that house them and, beyond their walls, by the system of laws and the imaginative works that justify and explain them. If Robert Blincoe's life-story created the climate responsible for the Reform Act of 1832, the act which invented the modern notion of paid employment, and provided the model for *Oliver Twist*, the novel that created the modern concept of the child, then Robert Blincoe is guilty on two accounts. Remember this, each time you visit the human resources department, or find yourself slack-jawed in front of *The Tweenies*: you are standing at the end of two grand stories, both of which began with my great-great-grandfather.

Since the Factory Acts of the early nineteenth century, work has been determined according to the hours one spends at work. Of course, today many of us are paid piece-rates, in a return to a medieval working system which we disguise under the name "freelancer". But the horizon and the framework of employment remains the factory or the office. These institutions shape every aspect of modern life, creating the labour movement, the trade unions, the concept of retirement, the huge pension funds that govern our economies, national insurance and through that the health system and the state pension. Everything.

The story of Robert Blincoe occupies such a

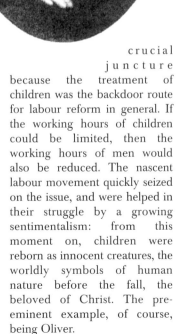

crucial juncture because the treatment of children was the backdoor route for labour reform in general. If the working hours of children could be limited, then the working hours of men would also be reduced. The nascent labour movement quickly seized on the issue, and were helped in their struggle by a growing sentimentalism: from this moment on, children were reborn as innocent creatures, the worldly symbols of human nature before the fall, the beloved of Christ. The pre-eminent example, of course, being Oliver.

Oliver bloody Twist.

If I had to be descended from anyone, did it have to be Oliver? Perhaps I ought to be honoured that the spirit of English literature courses through my veins, but I could have chosen a different character. The hero of Howard Jacobson's novel, *Peeping Tom*, all but falls into a coma in shock when he discovers he is the reincarnation of Thomas Hardy. I would give my right arm to be Thomas Hardy, or even Jude the Obscure – frankly, I would be happy to be one of Jude's kids. But you cannot choose your relatives. By inspiring Oliver Twist, Robert Blincoe stands as the model for all children's literary figures. One can see his outline in Charles Kingsley's *The Water Babies*, in Tom Brown and in J M Barrie's Lost Boys (though the name of Peter Pan's gang comes from a children's battalion that fought in the Paris Commune) and on to the pale hollow figures of contemporary children's fiction: the children that fly around with snowmen, ride aboard the Polar Express and play air hockey on broomsticks.

The mill-owners might have resisted reform, but were soon embroiled in a new struggle. As industrial reforms threw up a parallel movement for educational reform, the Anglican church and the mill-owners, who tended to belong to dissenting churches, were soon fighting over who would have the responsibility for the new schools. From most viewpoints,

this entire history is one of unrelieved progress: work hours are reduced, school hours extended, conditions are improved, literacy soars. But we should be suspicious, the story of constant improvement is a little too cosy to be believed.

The War on Work, if war we want, cannot be happy with reform. From the standpoint of the radical, reform does not ease a problem, it consolidates it. The long history of industrial reform has merely confirmed that "work" means going to work, surrendering our freedom of movement and action for the strictly regulated confines of the workplace. The labour movement has been complicitous in our bondage, and not merely from the reform-minded centre-left, but even from the radical fringes. The left has always organised around the workplace. The theoretical justification, from Marx onwards, is that the class struggle is essentially a struggle for the means of production – and where else can this be fought, other than in the workplace? The libertarian Left, bizarrely, has been even more fervent in binding us ever tighter to the work. Peter Kropotkin, the author of *Fields, Factories and Workshops*, envisaged a post-capitalist utopia in which the whole world was transformed into a work space. Kropotkin's work gave birth to syndicalism, the belief that society ought to be run from the shop-floor through the unions, an idea that reached its apogee in the Spanish Civil War, and never recovered from the syndicalists failure to defeat Franco's North African battalions, the least distinguished army in modern Europe.

From a classic Marxist-Leninist perspective, Robert Blincoe was a class traitor. After his expulsion from the Nottinghamshire mill at the age of twenty-two, he never again worked full-time for anyone but himself. After a few years as an itinerant mill hand, he set up as a cloth-picker – a kind of rag-and-bone merchant – and despite a short-spell in debtor's prison in Lancaster, built a thriving family business in Manchester with his wife. The later editions of the Memoirs includes an interview in which Blincoe describes the still poor conditions in the mills of Manchester, adding that he would never send his children to work in one, because they would surely end up crippled. Yet it is clear from this and other remarks, that Blincoe had nothing against child labour. It was fine for his children to work, as long as they worked for the family. Work and school co-existed: Blincoe credits his daughter with teaching him how to read, one of his two sons gained a scholarship to Cambridge and became an Anglican priest. This later story is a classic petty-bourgeois tale, Robert Blincoe is the shop-keeper who made good and saw his children prosper. It is, I think, a happy story. Family businesses are too often maligned: they may not have worked for Oedipus, but they turned out well for the Blincoes.

Robert Blincoe refused to organise as a worker, and chose instead to behave as though he were a boss. This may not have been the industrial proletariat's best strategy in the nineteenth century – who can say? – yet it provides a model for our own War on Work. The battle lines today are very different from the Victorian age when the private company, led by bloody-minded entrepreneurs, faced down mass ranks of strikers. Today, public corporations hold sway and our working lives are governed by employment law, tribunals and reconciliation services. Clearly we need to get militant, and that could mean acting more like bosses. The life of today's CEO is risk-free: they do not put their money in to the companies. The chief difference between the bosses and any other employees – aside from pay – is that they are never tied to the workplace. They take on multiple jobs, directorships and advisory roles. They are not policed by the Human Resources department, their most intimate biographical and medical details are never kept on file. The CEO is judged on productivity but how they choose to do this, that is left to their own discretion. In every important respect, the bosses are free. Only we, the workers, live our lives under a microscope, constrained to appear each day at the console or lathe and martyr our lives beneath strip-lights. We are doubly abused: as long as we are forbidden from following the bosses' example, organising our

"Work" means going to work, and surrendering our freedom to the strictly regulated confines of the workplace

own lives and even taking on multiple jobs, then our human rights are being violated, and our economic system is being distorted. We suffer twice, as individuals and as a society; we lose our personal freedom and the advantages of a free labour market.

If we wish to fight the War on Work, then fight it on better ground: in the courts not the tribunals, and in criminal cases, not according to employment law. Sabotage HR. Sue for the right to stay home. Let's be done with reform: until we can work the hours we choose, in the place we wish, then work will always stand in opposition to life, rather than a facet of who we are. If Robert Blincoe's story teaches us anything, it is that the drive to reform appealed to everyone except the person who inspired it. He wanted to stay home with the wife and kids. ✆

ST. JOHN'S AMBULANCE PIN CUSHION, RACHEL WILLIAMS, N. YORKSHIRE 1999

FOLK ART

Jeremy Deller **and** Alan Kane's collection of unsung creativity. Introduction by Tom Hodgkinson

What is folk art? Jeremy Deller, Bruce Haines and Alan Kane have spent the last few years travelling around the country and recording the creativity of people who would never consider themselves to be artists. Folk art is art that would never be pretentious enough to call itself art. For one thing, it is not on the market. For another, it is unsigned. Therefore it hasn't been made for profit or for ego. It has been made entirely for its own sake. "Art" so called is something done by other people, professionals; folk art is done by us, amateurs. Deller describes the work as "stuff we like". In this sense, it is in the tradition of the handicraft revival that William Morris pioneered in the late 19th century. Morris was appalled by the effects of the industrial revolution on the creativity of the people. Factory work and the division of labour removed creative activity from ordinary people and put it in the hands of a sort of artistic elite. He harked back to the medieval age, when the whole town would come together to create, for example, the cathedrals. Morris saw creativity at the heart of a whole life. "The pleasure which ought to go with the making of every piece of handicraft has for its basis the keen interest, which every healthy man takes in healthy life, and is compounded, it seems to me, chiefly of three elements – variety, hope of creation and the self-respect which comes of a sense of usefulness." The Folk Art Archive demonstrates that in spite of widespread mechanization and specialization, everyday acts of creation have not died and that the urge and the need to make things is still very much alive. It demonstrates that despite our contemporary money ethic, which says that it's not worth putting any effort into anything unless it is going to turn a profit, art for art's sake lives on. It shows that there is more to life than work and TV. The Folk Art archive is also a radical attack on that scourge of modern life: boredom. The philosopher Raoul Vaneigem (interviewed elsewhere in this issue) wrote in the 1960s that "boredom is literally killing us." He argued that everyday creativity was a way of attacking boredom and whatever else it is, none of the work here could be described as boring. ☯

The Folk Art archivists have gathered here pieces based on the theme of transport. The Folk Art Archive is showing from 12 May to 26 July at the Barbican Curve Gallery and then tours to Milton Keynes, Exeter and Walsall. See www.folkarchive.co.uk for more information.

SNOWDROP THE MECHANICAL ELEPHANT,
CRAB FAIR, EGREMONT 2004

DRAG RACER, EGREMONT, 2004

RURAL FREEDOM FIGHTER

COUNTRYSIDE ALLIANCE DEMONSTRATOR, WHITEHALL, LONDON 2002

KEITH RICHARDS PAINTING ON LORRY CAB, M2 KENT, 2003

W.M.D. found in PETERLEE, made for export to ISRAEL

MO OR D

Remember Rachel crushed to death,

paign

'all
all

nd and

rms,

onal law

' Gala
e

l badges £2
£2·50
50p

FREE
STINE

9,000 HOMES
DESTROYED
(W.M.D?)

VE
E

orrie, U.S. peace activist –
th.March, 2003.

COUNTRYSIDE ALLIANCE DEMONSTRATION, WHITEHALL, LONDON 2002

PARADE OF THE APPLE CART, EGREMONT, CUMBRIA, 2004

WEDDING CAR, DALSTON, 2004

OWL ROADSIDE BALE SCULPTURE, NR AMERSBURY, WILTSHIRE, 2005

RASTAFARIAN ILLUSTRATED CAR, LONDON 2002

MARI LLWYD IN A TAXI, LLANTRISANT, SOUTH WALES, 2000

HARD WORKING FAMILIES

Jack Thurston on why we must resist
New Labour's cult of hard work.
Illustrations by Sophie Lodge

The Labour Party will seek to win a third term of office with a claim to be on the side of Britain's "hard-working families". The expression "hard-working families" is by now a familiar feature of the political landscape. It peppered Labour's 2001 election manifesto and was spelt out in giant letters on the stage backdrop at the party's conference last autumn, dwarfing the delegates standing to address the party faithful. You will find it in speeches and articles by Cabinet ministers, backbench MPs and youthful political wannabes. It even bridges Britain's great political divide between the Prime Minister and his Chancellor. A Google search of the world wide web reveals 1,409 occurrences of the phrase in conjunction with Tony Blair. Gordon Brown is only marginally behind with 1,110 hits. Lacking any decent catch-phrases of their own, the Tories have lately adopted the expression, rather unimaginatively arguing "no,

New Labour's uncompromising message is rooted in the joyless Methodist preaching of the nineteenth century

no, no, don't listen to them, it's the Conservative Party, not Labour, that's the real friend of Britain's hard-working families".

Once a phrase becomes so entrenched in the political lexicon as to be happily used by every side, it is usually safe to dismiss it as hollowed out, meaningless and lacking any real policy content. But the idea of the "hard-working family", I regret to report, is no empty pleasantry. Rather, it forms the dark heart of New Labour's work-driven ideology and is well on the way to infecting the entire political establishment.

Writing in January's *Guardian*, Alan Milburn, the man who resigned from the Cabinet to spend more time with his family only to become bored after less than eighteen months, completed a remarkable about-turn. Now back in the Cabinet, Milburn is in charge of running the election campaign and writing the manifesto. Unsurprisingly, "hard-working families" loom large in his rhetoric. But he offers some revealing elaboration when he tells us that Labour's appeal to voters will be based on the idea that "if you play by the rules, you get a chance to progress". Milburn's own career path offers something by way of explanation and is a journey he shares with many in the current generation of Labour politicians. In the 1980s he flirted with the radical left and was involved in running a bookshop on Tyneside called Days of Hope (known to many at the time by a deliciously irresistible spoonerism Haze of Dope). Those freewheeling days were marked by electoral failure, political marginalization and a sense of permanent defeat. Only in the 1990s, once he had discovered the joys of hard work, traded the caftan for the sharp suit and nailed his flag to the mast of "new" Labour, did his political fortunes change. The message: dreamers are wasters; idleness is for losers. New Labour's uncompromising message is rooted in the joyless Methodist preaching of the nineteenth century. In New Labour's secular version, a devotion to God becomes a devotion to "personal prosperity" and it too relies upon the promise of future rewards in exchange for enduring today's privations. The party's theme

tune spells it out in the clearest of terms: *Things Can Only Get Better* (but just not yet).

As a political message it is devoid of the imagination for social transformation that we should expect from the Left. The obsession with "playing by the rules" reveals an intolerance for diversity, not the conventional notions of diversity in terms of who we are, but rather how we choose to live our lives. Of course, the Government is only too willing to set up commissions and task-forces and establish targets and quotas for diversity in gender, ethnicity and sexual orientation, but it does not accept that in any healthy society there must be room for people to break the rules or make up their own rules, challenge the system and refuse conformity.

British people work the longest hours in the European Union. More and more, our identities are defined by what we do at work. Yet we lag behind in terms of productivity. Treasury spin-doctors present the image of Chancellor Gordon Brown up at the crack of dawn, banging on the doors of the Treasury with armfuls of ideas on how to reduce the "productivity gap" with other nations. It must torment his Presbyterian soul that France is higher up the productivity league than the UK even though the French still enjoy two hour lunches and eight weeks of holiday a year. In short, they fit their work around their lives. New Labour thinks we should fit our lives around our work.

If the Chancellor were to take just a moment to understand how it is that productivity is calculated (I would recommend a hammock as an excellent venue for such contemplation), then he would stop fretting. Productivity is simply a measure of a country's Gross Domestic Product (GDP) divided by the number of hours its people work. If you accept the basic economic principle of diminishing marginal returns (that we tend to get more done at the start of day than at the end when we are tired and fed up), by working fewer hours, a nation will increase its productivity.

The industrial era is defined by the continual invention of new labour-saving devices, from the spinning jenny to the iMac. Dazzling technological progress gave us the idea that one day it would be possible for us all to relax while an army of willing robots did all the work, freeing us to enjoy all the new-found leisure time denied our forebears, slaves to the forces of economic necessity. That day looks as far off now as it ever was. Instead, we've been sold a future in which technology simply expands the amount of work we can do and drives a consumer culture that equates consumption with happiness and personal fulfilment.

Another reason people feel they have be "hard-working" is that the work culture has caused the housing market to go completely insane. Escalating house prices mean we have to work like dogs to earn more to pay the rent or the mortgage. Higher earnings drive up house prices. A vicious circle that benefits nobody but estate agents. Now if we all worked a little less, earned a little less, house prices would return to a sensible level, and we'd all actually have the time on our hands to enjoy spending some time at home, taking it easy.

So how did we get into this mess? And what can be done about it? Of course it is unfair to blame Tony Blair and his ministers for the entire edifice of advanced industrial capitalism. But politicians do bear responsibility for peddling a work ethic that reveres paid employment and denigrates anything else (with the exception of shopping, keep-fit and DIY, each of which so-called leisure activities bears a frightening resemblance to work).

The problem is that New Labour can't resist the desire to build a world in its own image. And if you take a close look at the kind of people who make up the New Labour project, this should be a major cause for concern for anyone who wants a life where there's enough time to smell a flower, eat a long slow meal or gaze at the sky. Even the most well-motivated politicians are unusual people driven by a rare desire for the adrenalin, drama and excitement of a life in the public eye. To succeed in politics you have to work damned hard at it. And here is the problem in a nutshell. The people running the country are different from the rest of us. In fact, their overblown appetite for work is the very reason they are running the country and not us.

If you take a look at the lad culture of New Labour *apparatchiks*, you will find that the only passion that may challenge their love of politics is their devotion to football. For many of these types, the "weekend" means the couple of hours it takes to go "down the Arsenal" on a Saturday afternoon. I wonder if we'd have a more humane politics if our politicians were instead advised by a corps of spin-doctors and policy wonks devoted to more relaxed pastimes. Crown Green Bowls, perhaps. Or leisurely cycle touring, in the Edwardian manner.

And if they did, what kind of policies could we expect them to dream up? How about a statutory right to a four day week, in exchange for less pay? Or giving tax breaks to job-sharers as a way of increasing employment? If we switched taxation from earnings to consumption, we could all work less yet earn the same amount, freeing up the time we need to do fun things that don't cost money. Unfortunately policies like these are an abomination to a political class that works hard, plays hard and expects us to do the same. It is time to resist the totalitarian vision of the "hard-working family".

Jack Thurston was a Government special adviser from 1999 to 2001.

If we switched taxation from earnings to consumption, we could all work less yet earn the same amount

WAR NOT WORK

Richard Donkin on how, in medieval times, bloodshed and violence was a good way of avoiding drudgery. Illustrations by Walshworks

I recently saw evidence of my ancestry imprinted in the results of a personality questionnaire. It provided a cultural match with people who live in different parts of the world. My responses placed me among the Scandinavians. This was no surprise since I can trace my family roots back to the north-east coast of England, a part of the world that was first ravaged, then settled by Viking invaders.

At some time in the Donkin family past, then, before the Venerable Bede was moved to write his history of England, there must have been a sexual encounter between an Anglo Saxon maiden and some bearded sea-fairing Kirk Douglas lookalike intent on rape and pillage. Except the Kirk Douglas comparison is unlikely since the dimpled chin is a dominant gene passed down from father to son over the centuries and I don't have a dimple.

Not all Vikings were violent marauders but it seems logical to assume that to book your slot in a long boat you would need to demonstrate at least a hint of ferocity when the occasion demanded it. Or maybe supplies of the mushroom *Amanita Muscaria* (Fly Agaric) were plentiful enough to turn the mildest Nordic into a shield-biting Beserker.

Where I come from a few pints of Tetley Bitter can induce similar effects. Alternatively, modern living has given us road rage, passenger rage and kill-your-neighbour rage. Indeed we can extend this list to other tantrum-inducing stimulus such as plastic wrapping, video recorders, ticket machines and Linda Barker's voice.

But no matter how angry we become it is difficult to resist the equilibrium of domesticity that has

invaded our working lives. So are we living in a natural state or could we be denying a latent preference for lengthy periods of idleness punctuated by brief explosions of aggression?

This, after all, was the behaviour of the Germanic tribesmen observed by Tacitus in *Germanica*. As Roman society degenerated, the German tribes, north of the Rhine, were biding their time and taking it easy. While the so-called barbarian, apparently, was action personified in battle, once back at home stretched out in front of the hearth he was more of a Ricky Tomlinson playing the idle father figure in *The Royle Family*.

According to Tacitus: "When the state has no war to manage the German mind is sunk in sloth. The chase does not provide sufficient employment. The time is passed in sleep and gluttony. The intrepid warrior, who in the field braved every danger, becomes in time of peace a listless sluggard. The management of his house and lands he leaves to the women, to the old men, and the infirm. He himself lounges in stupid repose, by a wonderful diversity of nature exhibiting in the same man the most inert aversion to labour, and the fiercest principle of action."

An aversion to work in the warrior code is not confined to the Germanic tribes. It was just as apparent in the age of chivalry when knighthood reflected a status beyond that of the common labourer or tradesman. Chaucer's "varry parfit gentile knight" in the *Cantebury Tales* is recognised for his good manners and courage in battle, not for hard work. When Richard I acceded to the throne of England the last thing he wanted to do was administer matters of state. Instead, at the drop of a helmet, he raced off to the Holy Land to get in some fighting.

The division between war and work has a history that goes back to the dawn of humanity. While the earliest implements known to have been used by our ancestors were hand axes – simple cutting tools – it is worth recalling that Stanley Kubrick, the film director, envisaged the original spark of inspiration that divided man and ape as the discovery, not of the tool, but of the weapon.

Could we be denying a preference for idle periods punctuated with aggression?

Leaving aside Arthur C. Clarke's novel suggestion that we might owe our origins to some alien intelligence, the theme that provided a continual source of fascination for Kubrick, was man's propensity for violence. Hence the scene at the beginning of *2001: A Space Odyssey* when those unconvincing screen apes are engaged in aggressive group behaviour before one of them finds a large bone. In a single giant leap of intellectual creativity the bone becomes a club which is used to bludgeon a competitor. The dramatic crescendo of Richard Strauss's *Thus Spake Zarathustra* announces the triumphant ape's conquering gesture as it hurls the bone in to the air before it is transformed majestically in to a rotating space station moving dreamily to the strains of the *Blue Danube* waltz. Complete bollocks, but great cinema.

There is very little evidence in the fossil record to suggest that the first people displayed such warlike traits. On the contrary most discoveries from the stone age point to a relatively peaceful and co-operative existence among the communities of Neolithic Europe, trading stone tools and banding together to create ambitious megalith structures such as the circles at Stonehenge and Avebury in Wiltshire and the stone-lined avenues at Carnac in Brittany.

But there is evidence that the modern definition of work as something we would rather not be doing was framed at this time. This was the era when nomadic bands had begun to plant crops that created surpluses thanks to the invention of the grindstone. The farm and the grindstone transformed the hunter-gathering life and evolved something less satisfying than tearing around the countryside in pursuit of wild beasts. It created work and domesticity. The biggest beneficiaries were women who no longer had to cart their children on their backs between camps. So it seems logical to assume that women were expected to do much of this new drudge-work.

At least this would have been the case before someone had the idea to profit by making war rather than raising crops, and to spare some captives for a life of slavery. Warfare among men was a natural progression from the hunt since conquest was and remains one of the most effective ways of acquiring wealth, possessions and status.

In fact for Attila the Hun, the acquisition of wealth was a by-product of the conquering which is what he really enjoyed. Attila defied the adage that you can't take it with you when you die. He was buried with many of his riches and his grave with all its booty remains one of the world's great hidden treasures.

You can see the same Attila tendencies today in the behaviour of tycoons like Rupert Murdoch and Philip Green. For these corporate warriors their stimulation is not so much work but conquest. Corporate empire building has bred an obsession for deal-making which shares many of the same characteristics found in displays of military aggression.

In fact work has never featured strongly among the world's élite. The Athenians, who had slaves to do nearly all their chores, did not have a specific word for work. They had *ergon* that referred to farm labour and they used *ponos* to refer to some painful task. But otherwise they would use the opposite of *scholia*, the word for leisure. This is *ascholia*, literally, "not leisure". At least the Athenians took an interest in administration. The Spartans were focussed primarily on military service to the exclusion of almost everything else since they got helots to do their slave work.

The modern day Spartan is the gym-obsessed, smart-suited executive who takes working lunches of fruit and water, jogs to the office and looks down on the swarming helots commuting to and from their city-based terminals.

This is hardly the behaviour of the Visigoth and certainly not of the Hun before whom even the Visigoths took to their heels. So where did the reputation for idleness emerge among the Germanic tribes? Tacitus does not single out any particular ethnic group but had he done so he would probably have settled on the Gepids, a Germanic tribe that had originated in Scandinavia.

The Gepids never managed to create their own state, perhaps because they could never be bothered to do so. But they did gain favour with Attila and fought alongside him at the battle of Chalons in 451. Among the Goths, however, they had earned a reputation for being somewhat tardy. In fact when one of the not infrequent tribal migrations was arranged they turned up late for the rendezvous with the other tribes at the mouth of the Vistula. Somehow they managed to get as far as Sirmium (now Sremska Mitrovica) in the Danube valley before what power they had was wiped out by the Avars.

Should we conclude from Tacitus's observations that both war and leisure have been perceived historically, at least by men, as attractive bedfellows that can prove far more alluring than the prospect of work? The Duke of Wellington's remark that the battle of Waterloo was won on the playing fields of Eton might have been closer to the truth than even he could have appreciated.

This would explain why there was no shortage of fresh recruits among the belligerents at the outbreak of the First World War. And what did both sides do during their first Christmas in the trenches? They had a game of football in no-man's land – much more fun than mending the wire.

The Futurists – that group of Italian artists that introduced the cubist painting style into their images of fast cars, aeroplanes and trains – were among the first to sign up for the war before they realised that warfare had an ugly side.

This mutual relationship between excitement and danger must surely explain the growth in dangerous sports among the young. Is there really such a difference between the surfing bum, loafing on the beach, before dashing out to ride a wave and the laid back Germanic warrior resting between campaigns? What did Battle of Britain fighter pilots do between sorties but loaf around in deck chairs? All would agree that serious action demands compensating idleness. As Isaac Newton discovered in his third law of motion, for every action there is an equal and opposite reaction.

Few would argue that there is a certain nobility in the dynamism of extreme sports but it cannot replicate the emotional spectrum of shared experience during, say, the Charge of the Light Brigade or among the English bowmen at Agincourt. "We would not die in that man's company that fears his fellowship to die with us," says Shakespeare's Henry V on the eve of battle,

work has never featured strongly among the world's elite

addressing those he calls his "band of brothers". As Shakespeare knew, the depth of friendship to be found in shared adversity is rare and precious.

Of those who have never experienced warfare I doubt if there is a man alive who does not wonder how he would behave under fire. Just as there are those who understand the joy of war. This is not to dignify or celebrate conflict but to place it on a different level of experience than anything that can be found in a steady job other than, perhaps, working for the emergency services. Neither should we think of higher or lower planes, but of the stronger, some might say Nietzschean (well Nietzsche would) sense of living that pulses within our veins the nearer we approach that sharp divide between life and death.

That's the irony of living life to the full. The closer we step towards the edge of our existence the more we may appreciate the vitality and beauty of life. ◉

Richard Donkin is the author of *Blood, Sweat and Tears, the Evolution of Work* (Texere)

PLAY AWAY

Pat Kane wants to forget work and muck about instead. Here he imagines setting up a Play Foundation, in opposition to Will Hutton's Drudgery Foundation

I once went for a high-powered "think-dinner" with Will Hutton, *Observer* columnist and director of the Work Foundation, in a hotel overlooking Hyde Park. As the author of a then-impending book called *The Play Ethic*, I was intrigued by the invite.

Two of his colleagues were launching a paper called "Transforming Work". I'd read it beforehand, and had cringed a little at its primary objective: to establish the word "workful" as a legitimate way to describe the meaningful, worthwhile job. It sounded like an attempt to colonise what we mean by "playful" – activity that we choose to do, guided by joy and absorption –

After a certain amount of heat and light, we blinked pleasantly at each other over the coffee

and of course it was.

One of the paper's authors, Richard Reeves, had written a book called *Happy Mondays*, about how we secretly love our jobs – he believed they were more vital forms of community and purpose than we find at home or in leisure. As a musician, hacker and loving father, who tries to maintain a flexible relationship between my technology, social situations and passions, I couldn't have disagreed more. So as the wine was poured and the chicken rolled out, I expected to be in a bit of a feud for the next few hours.

It wasn't too fractious, as it turned out. But our differences were profound. The Work Foundation people were interested in closing the gap between the structure and ritual that necessarily composes any organisation or company, and the ever rising dissatisfaction of workers with those constrictions. Their healing advice was: a little more self-determination of work schedules and granting of sabbaticals on the one hand, and some warmer, more enabling language from management on the other.

I was interested in where those aspirations might lead, given the opportunity – what new forms of acting-together might they create? The musicians or artists that come together to form a great band or company; the techies and nerds who obsess about an innovation that changes the rules of an area of society or economy (the internet being the classic example); even those who put emotion, values and relationships first in their lives, and shape their money-and-power necessities around that commitment. They were interested in workers, in short, and I was interested in players. After a certain amount of heat and light, we blinked pleasantly at each other over the coffee.

"Perhaps," said Hutton with a certain post-prandial impishness, "you should think about establishing your own Play Foundation. We'd certainly welcome the competition. Like to see how well you'd do."

It's a thought – and in the spirit of idle speculation encouraged by this publication, let me try and flesh it out. Foundations, as far as I've observed, are entities that have been given considerable sums of interest-generating cash so that an intellectual or cultural agenda can be sustainably pursued. A Play Foundation would therefore be dedicated to research and promoting an agenda for play – as a way of being, acting and thinking in the world – which would be just as ambitious as Hutton-and-pals' agenda for work.

What's the agenda for such a foundation? A few theses:

Too many of us are happy to accept a crippling dualism in our lives. Our willingness to come together to make objects or services that enhance and

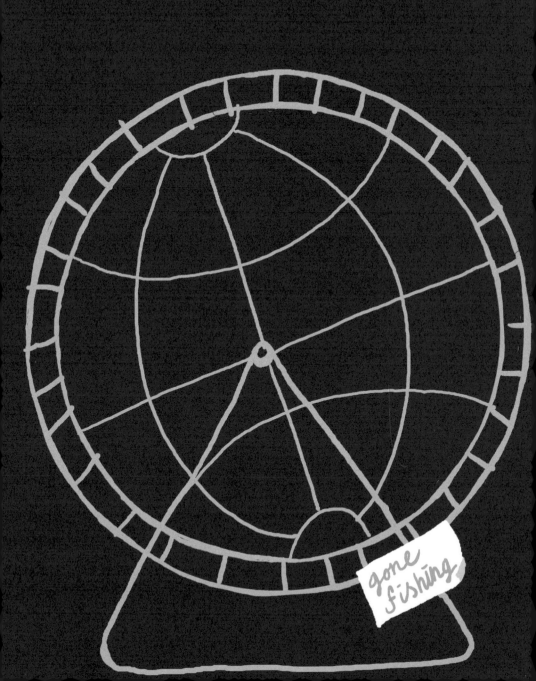

improve our society shouldn't be confined to the term "work". And our inexhaustible human urge to express ourselves, to dream of different worlds and futures, to seek out new experiences and relationships – all this shouldn't be confined to the realm of "leisure" or "recreation". How can we integrate these two human impulses – that is, our ability to produce, and our capacity to imagine?

I believe that play, and particularly the notion of the player, can be a new and unifying force in our lives. The first thing we need to do is to make our understanding of the term much more profound. We need to shrug off the Puritan legacy – "the soul's play-day is the devil's work-day" – that has confined play to childishness at best, and deviance at worst.

The word "play" itself has a surprising etymology. It comes from the Indo-European term *dlegh*, meaning "to engage, to exercise oneself". Play is essentially about active, mobile and energetic individuals, existing in a dynamic relationship with others. Hardly a trivial or silly definition.

Look at biology and psychology, and we can see how play is as essential to human development as work – arguably more so. It is through early play that we complex mammals build up the essential skills for survival and flourishing. And as our societies move further and further away from scarcity and into affluence, these core skills of play – communicating, interacting, imagining, experimenting – become more central and vital to our adult lives, not more marginal.

I think play can mostly replace what we're currently describing as work. But we have to be much more sophisticated in our understanding of play, and much less moralistic about our idea of work, for that

to happen. It's almost a truism now that information capitalism seeks to press an ever wider spectrum of our capacities and sensibilities into its service – with, as the record shows, a very mixed success rate (witness everything from absenteeism to hackerism). I don't think we're very far away – indeed, we might be at the start – of a major revolt against the very notion of "work" as any kind of description of the variety of ways that a conscious, self-developing info-citizen might add value to this world.

My aim with *The Play Ethic* is to give this revolt one possible constructive (rather than cynical or despairing) outlet – a positive identity of the "player", and player-friendly institutions, as opposed to the worker and the work ethic. It might be a way to align our burgeoning sense of potential, with a realm of actions that in some way answers that.

Of course there is a limit to play – yet it's more about occupying a different point on the spectrum of human "response-abilities", to coin a phrase. That aspect of work that implies duty, a commitment to reciprocate in a steadfast manner with others, I think should be called "care" instead. The Play Ethic often counterposes the "work-leisure" tension, and the "work-life balance", with the "play-care continuum".

A players' society recognizes that playerhood might involve a long fall from the high-wire (or even the low-wire) of info-age opportunity and options, and that we have to devise systems and cultures of support and well-being to enable people to bounce back to the fray: players need social trampolines rather than social nets. Contrary to the libertarian ludicists I do think players need some level of collective support for when their risky, openness-embracing endeavours fail or flail. So between a strong play ethic and a strong care ethic, for me the work ethic simply dissolves. The work ethic represses what needs to be unleashed (play), and instrumentalizes what needs to be deeply felt (care).

Enough! (After that, go read the book). So what would this agenda mean in terms of a foundation's priorities?

Gather together the cross-disciplinary scholarship on play – from biology to computer science, from culture to sports, from philosophy to economics. It's outrageous that such a global, cross-species, cross-class, cross-generational phenomenon does not have the very basis of a scholarly investment. Play, in all its forms, needs to be taken seriously (no paradox) – and we'd start here.

Identify those social groups who were already explicitly using and identifying with play – in values and practices – and both study and support them. There is a powerful social alliance waiting to be forged between all those who identify themselves as players – gamesters and hackers, entrepreneurs both social and private, children and parents, activists and artists. What kind of society could they imagine, if they all started to talk to each other?

Investigate the grounds of play – what would a players' infrastructure look like? We know how to reproduce the conditions that keep us as workers – wages, mortgages, nuclear families, overtime, compensatory consumption. Can we begin to investigate what institutions and practices we would need to sustain our identity as players? What common resources, what access to facilities, what kinds of learning and housing and moving?

Play with what we've discovered. A good foundation/think-tank pumps its

Between a strong play ethic and a strong care ethic, the work ethic simply dissolves

ideas into practice as quickly as it can. So we'd have a website, means to distribute ideas onto every available platform – from mobile phones to digital TV – and a great press-and-publicity person. Like those Institute of Ideas people, except funkier.

It would also, of course, be housed in some fantastically charismatic old factory space in either Glasgow or London, be brimming with the latest Macs and the fattest bandwidth, and have an ambience somewhere between a health spa, a hip restaurant, an arts lab and a nightclub (with an ace play foundation attached).

Budget? About £1 million a year for five years. Likelihood? From tiny articles in renegade publications are outrageous connections sometimes made… And I promise you: Will Hutton will be the first one in for a cup of Vodka'n'Chai. 🍥

Pat Kane is the author of
The Play Ethic: A Manifesto for a Different Way of Living (Macmillan)
Contact him at:
patkane@theplayethic.com or see
www.theplayethic.com

PASSIVE RESISTANCE

Yahia Lababidi on Herman Melville's character Bartleby, the man who preferred not to.
Illustrations by Marc Baines

Herman Melville published his first short story *Bartleby, the Scrivener: A Story of Wall Street* in 1853, anonymously. By that time, the author already had behind him seven years of novel writing, culminating in his great work of allegory: *Moby-Dick*. Republished in 1856, under the author's name and an abbreviated title, *Bartleby* is a miniature masterpiece, all the more captivating for its evocation of the uncanny. The enduring fascination it exerts is that of the cipher, as represented by the enigmatic character of the anti-hero, Bartleby, a strangely doomed figure of unfathomable depths lurking behind an inscrutable surface. As the story charts the gradual exasperation and emotional bafflement of his employer, our perception of Bartleby ever-so-faintly shifts, from strangely helpless to obscurely sinister.

The story begins well enough. The elderly narrator, an unambitious lawyer and Bartleby's employer is keenly observant and sympathetically tolerant of the eccentricities of human nature as manifested by his law-copyists. He faithfully renders their

idiosyncrasies in a loving and droll drawl, before lingering on the biography of Bartleby, "one of those beings of whom nothing is ascertainable." One day, in answer to an advertisement, Bartleby appears at his office like an apparition: "pallidly neat, pitiably respectable, incurably forlorn." He soon proceeds to gorge himself on documents, only cheerlessly. By the third day however, in response to an ordinary request to examine a paper with his employer, Bartleby first utters his inexplicable (and soon to become maddening) mantra: I would prefer not to. Rallying his stunned faculties, our narrator finds he is incapable of responding to this bizarre reply delivered with such perfect comportment. He may as well be cross with his bust of Cicero, he reasons. A few days later, summoned to a similar request, Bartleby again mildly repeats his startling reply, and gently takes his leave. Yet, somehow, Bartleby's dispassionate weirdness endears him to his employer, and he is left to retreat to his "hermitage," a high green folding screen in the corner of the room with a window facing on to a brick wall.

In time, the narrator comes to pity Bartleby's ascetic existence, living like a monk of an unnamed order, never dining, never leaving the office, and concludes that his eccentricities must be involuntary. He fears that if he were to turn him away Bartleby would surely find a less indulgent employer, and keeping him becomes a question of conscience. Thus, in his superhuman effort to humour Bartleby's perverse willfulness, his

employee comes to enjoy strange privileges and exemptions. Yet there are times when, prey to an all-too-human need for a reaction, any reaction, our narrator is irritated by his employee's "unalterableness of demeanor" and "great stillness". Early for church one Sunday he decides to pass by his office only to find that Bartleby, in an unusual state of tattered *dishabillé*, would "prefer not to" let him enter as he is "deeply engaged". Not without a certain impotent rebellion, the narrator slinks away from his own door. He returns later, out of curiosity, to discover (from belongings left behind) that Bartleby has been living in his office. Contemplating the sheer friendlessness and solitude this implies, he is overcome by a "fraternal melancholy" for the "pallid copyist". Yet by the mystery of emotions and the magic of moods, a deeper meditation on Bartleby's morbid condition causes melancholy to recoil into fear, and pity to slip into revulsion. Registering this new-found visceral understanding, the narrator decides to dismiss his unwholesome employee. But, first he must master his own superstitions at forsaking this "forlornest of mankind".

At some point in the story, Bartleby decides to take up the indefensible position of blankly declining to do any more writing, indulging only in his "dead wall revelry" all day, with dull glazed eyes The narrator, desperately, provides him with the excuse that his eyes must be ailing and exempts him from working for some days, only to have his employee confirm to him that he has permanently given up copying. Nevertheless, Bartleby stays on "useless as a necklace, but afflictive to bear," not unlike Coleridge's albatross in *The Rime of the Ancient Mariner*, and invested with the same allegorical gravitas and sense of foreboding. "A bit of a wreck in the mid Atlantic" the narrator helplessly notes of Bartleby. By now though, his compassion is laced with a deep unease and he issues a six day ultimatum during which time Bartleby must unconditionally leave the Office. And, yet, peeping behind the screen on the sixth day, there was Bartleby. "You must go," repeats the narrator, good-naturedly offering him $20 and inviting him to write if he should need anything. "I would prefer not to" is his employees' only reply, standing in silence "like the last column of some ruined temple."

The next morning, following frantic conjecture as to whether or not Bartleby has finally vacated the premises, the narrator returns to his office. "Not yet, I'm occupied," comes the familiar voice from within. Submitting to the scrivener's "wondrous ascendancy", he retreats with a mixture of perplexity and nervous resentment. But pity triumphs and as a result of his spiritual readings and temperament, our narrator experiences a sublimely ridiculous epiphany. He must accept Bartleby as predestined from eternity, and his mission in life to furnish him with office room. This generosity of spirit, alas, is fated not to last. Whispers of wonder over the strange creature he keeps, abound among his professional acquaintances and spark his own dark anticipation to overthrow the "intolerable incubus". The only way to rid himself of this "ghost" he decides is to change offices, which he does, albeit in terror that Bartleby might return to haunt him. Instead, it is the incensed landlord and tenants of his abandoned place of business who pay him a visit. They urge him to reason with Bartleby, who sits perched on the stair banisters by day and sleeps in the entrance hall by night, to everyone's consternation. Relenting to a thinly-veiled

> "Either you must do something, or something must be done to you." "No, I would prefer not to make any change," offers Bartleby

threat of public scandal, the narrator returns to present Bartleby with this necessary life choice: "Either you must do something, or something must be done to you." "No, I would prefer not to make any change," offers Bartleby, and our narrator flees the scene and town.

Upon his return, he finds a note. Bartleby has been removed by the police as a vagrant, taken to a prison known as the Tombs, and the narrator is summoned to make a statement. In prison, he finds Bartleby alone in a quiet yard facing a high wall, and their exchange is strained, defensive on the narrator's side and accusatory on Bartleby's. Before leaving, the narrator requests that particular attention be extended to his ex-employee (the best dinner, etc…) but Bartleby does not dine at all. When the narrator returns a few days later he finds him huddled at the base of the wall, in a kind of fetal position, and dead. Before parting with the reader, the narrator volunteers that if this tale should stir curiosity as to Bartleby's past, he shares in it. Ultimately, he must profess ignorance of this "man by nature and misfortune prone to pallid hopelessness."

At this point, several questions pose

themselves. Why is this man by nature and misfortune prone to hopelessness? Is he a casualty of the workplace, assaulted by pointlessness, or does he take refuge in the wearisome or lethargic to drain himself of some inner poison? Meaning, who introduced the hopelessness, Bartleby or the Office? And, what does he mean by his confounding mantra: I would prefer not to? Prefer not to what exactly? And, prefer to do what, instead? Existentially, what does this position entail: to do nothing and prefer not to make any change? To approach these questions, we may try to reconstruct an imaginary past to account for this unaccountable life: its quiet despair, its irrefutable sorrow, its ambiguous pain. In short, me must discover "what went wrong, what wound it expressed, what injury not to be healed. What had the man had, to make him by the loss of it so bleed, and yet live?" These words are from a short story by Henry James, *The Beast in the Jungle*. They occur to the protagonist as he passes a stranger in a cemetery, catching his eye. And, they may serve to frame our inquiry of the living-death that is Bartleby, with his entombed spirit, undying and unliving, wandering in the land of shades.

If existentially speaking, life may be likened to standing before a blank canvas, and living as filling that space, then what can be made of the proposition of refusing to engage? Or, to put it differently, if in response to our thrownness-into-being (Heidegger's words) we decide not to get up, walk or walk away? To shrug off the responsibility to participate is to reject life itself. It is the nihilist impulse personified, the very embodiment of negation. For, in actively rejecting everything, is it not Nothing that is passively sought? "Nothing is more real than nothing,"

offers Beckett, a literary Bartleby given to his own endgames, and condemned to life in his way. The narrator of Beckett's *The End* may well be speaking for Bartleby when he describes himself as, "without the courage to end or the strength to go on." Something of this nothingness infiltrates Bartleby, saps his strength and is at the heart of his inertia. For, with despair as with night-vision, the eyes soon grow accustomed to the dark.

Greek poet, Constantine Cavafy, is another example of an artist with such night-vision. In one poem, "Walls", we find him imperceptibly walled-in and in another, "The Windows", he is shutting out the "new tyranny of the light". His poem *The City* – with its hissing hopelessness, paralysis of will, early surrender and ashen gloom – is not unlike the mental space inhabited by Bartleby:

New lands you will not find, you will not find other seas.
The city will follow you. You will roam the same
streets. And you will age in the same neighborhoods;
in these same houses you will grow gray.
Always you will arrive in this city. To another land -- do not hope --
there is no ship for you, there is no road.
As you have ruined your life here
in this little corner, you have destroyed it in the whole world.

This bleak world view of life as inescapable sentence is also suggested in Rilke's poem, *The Panther*:
His vision, from the constantly passing bars,
has grown so weary
that it cannot hold anything else.
It seems to him there are a thousand bars;
and behind the bars,
no world.

As he paces in cramped circles, over and
over, the movement of his
powerful soft strides is like a ritual dance
around a center in which
a mighty will stands paralyzed.

Returning to Bartleby, pacing in cramped circles around a centre in which his will stands paralyzed, we must again ask why this is so. Is his will spoilt by misuse, disuse or abuse? Is it ravaged by a savage boredom? Is his imagination starved, his mind malnourished? Rilke's answer to this corrosive paralysis is the opposite of Bartleby's, namely, affirmation: Whoever does not affirm at some time or other with a definite resolve – yes, jubilate at – the terribleness of life, never takes possession of the unutterable powers of our existence; he merely walks at the edge; and when the decision is made eventually, he will have been neither one of the living nor one of the dead.

And in fact if it is the work that has depleted Bartleby's resources, then why does he stay? Why do people stay in occupations, relations, and spaces (inner and outer landscapes) that cease to nourish and sustain, or worse, never did? Stuck in their own mud, their wheels vainly spinning, why do people form spiritually deadening habits? What proves their undoing: which loss, what slight, what cumulative weariness or disenchantment? These are questions tied up with what is deep and unreasoning, questions of self-worth, or perhaps some perceived and invisible crime that is being atoned for.

Philip Larkin, a poet of bittersweet defeat, much of whose energy was drained (by his own admission) running a university library for decades, is in a position to answer some of these questions. In his poem, *Toads*, he sardonically interrogates himself:

Why should I let the toad work
Squat on my life?
Can't I use my wit as a pitchfork
And drive the brute off?

For something sufficiently toad-like
Squats in me, too;
Its hunkers are heavy as hard luck,
And cold as snow,
...
I don't say, one bodies the other
One's spiritual truth;
But I do say it's hard to lose either,
When you have both.

In another poem of his, tellingly entitled *Poetry of Departures*, the fifth-hand news of the "audacious, purifying elemental move" of someone who "chucked up everything and just cleared off" suffices to help Larkin stay on, albeit with envious resignation.

Undoubtedly, there is a deep-seated fear at bottom of this great unwillingness to engage, change, leave and start again. Kafka, who in his letters to *fiancé* Milena, agrees that he "may sometimes look like a bribed defender of [his] fear", is another connoisseur of things he would "prefer not to do". A law clerk throughout his life, and writer by night, he sums up his existence in his diaries as "a hesitation before birth." Yet in another letter, this time to friend Max Brod, he is capable of seeing his situation with more clarity and courage. Speaking of a hypothetical writer, Kafka says: "...he has a terrible fear of dying because he has not yet lived... what is essential to life is only to forgo complacency, to move into the house instead of admiring it and hanging garlands around it." This recognition of complacency and moving into life's house is precisely what Bartleby seems incapable of.

In the course of the story, the complacency of Melville's scrivener becomes complete, monumental. He had arrived already half-wasted, a guardian of some obscure pain, and dangerously flirting with non-being. His "great stillness", which alternately fascinated and rattled his employer, may hold the key to the mystery.

After reading Nietzsche's *Thus Spake Zarathustra*, author Paul Lanzky decided to seek out the philosopher who was living in complete isolation in Italy. Despite being struck by his humanity and amiability, Lanzky notes: "Nietzsche's being displayed so much naivete ...so much wise devotion to the most modest and world-remote life, that to me the catastrophe [his madness] seemed inavoidable... this longing for stillness, indeed this temporary reveling in the idyllic, suddenly seemed ...like a weariness of soul..."

Analyzing Gogol's genius in *The Overcoat*, Vladimir Nabokov also touches on some of the themes that pertain to Bartleby. "The absurd," he writes, "has as many shades and degrees as the tragic... You cannot place a man in an absurd situation if the whole world he lives in is absurd." The real "message" of the story, he tells us, is that "something is very wrong and all men are mild lunatics engaged in pursuits that seem to them very important while an absurdly logical force keeps them at their futile jobs." Speaking of the hero of *The Overcoat*, Nabokov comes close to summarizing Melville's anti-hero when he says: "[He] is absurd because he is pathetic, because he is human ... that meek little clerk, a ghost, a visitor from some tragic depths who by

chance happened to assume the disguise of a petty official." After reading Gogol, Nabokov admits that one's eyes may become "gogolized", with fragments of Gogol's world surfacing in unforeseen places.

Yet, Bartleby's ancestors and heirs are not merely literary, nor is he the exclusive property of a select band of eccentrics. Rather, he is the patron saint of the civil servant, the dispirited automatons of an absurd workplace, the insulted and injured of the world. In other words, all who "measure out their lives in coffee spoons" (Prufrock's famous phrasing) in demoralizing circumstances, performing tedious tasks that, quite frankly, they would prefer not to. In this sense, Bartleby may be read as a cautionary tale concerning the perils of passive resistance and spiritual stagnation; the dust, rust or moss that gathers from staying in place. "The man who never alters his opinion/Is like standing water/And breeds reptiles of the mind" writes William Blake. Resentment, bitterness, complacency, paralysis, or hopelessness are such examples. In that sense, Bartleby may be said to exist in everyone, in various concentrations. Ah Bartleby, Ah humanity! ◉

QUIET RIOT

Edward Sage rounds up the latest anti-work movements from the US and beyond

There's a revolution going on. And it's fighting a global epidemic of meaningless drudgery and long, long hours. Over the past few years, a plethora of websites, magazines and movements have sprung up which all have the common aim of pointing out just how hard we work and just how ludicrous the situation has become. In America, particularly, people are working harder than ever. Sociologist Juliet B. Schor has partly attributed this culture of overwork to a new type of consumerism. During the US economic boom of the 1990s, people began forming their consumer aspirations by looking to the rich, rather than to those of a similar socio-economic status, and this new desire for luxury and affluence has resulted in people wanting to work longer hours. But Schor also argues that there are "systematic pressures within the production process, coming from the profitability strategies of employers, which translate productivity growth into greater output and increased incomes rather than shorter hours of work." Workers are no longer getting the option to reduce their hours, and with more people competing for a limited number of salaried jobs, employers are able to demand more. In the hourly job sector, the ongoing decrease in wages has resulted in people being forced to increase their hours to maintain their income. Schor has revealed that over the last two decades working hours have increased by the equivalent of one month per year. Three quarters of the workforce work more than forty hours a week, and a third work over fifty hours.

But there is a backlash. A global anti-work movement seems to be gathering force, and here we present some of the groups we've found.

TAKE BACK YOUR TIME (USA/CANADA)

Take Back Your Time (timeday.org) is a nationwide initiative which aims to challenge "the epidemic of overwork, over-scheduling and time famine that now threatens our health, our families and relationships, our communities and our environment". They have designated 24 October as Take Back Your Time Day, and each year thousands of Americans take the day off to protest. The date, which falls about nine weeks before the end of the year, highlights the fact that Americans work an average of nine weeks (350 hours) a year more than Western Europeans.

THE SIMPLE LIVING NETWORK (USA)

The Simple Living Network's website (simpleliving.net) offers tools, examples and contacts for simple, healthy and restorative living. Founded in January 1996, the network has grown to become a focus point for those who are dedicated to simple living. The Simplicity Forum, part of the network, is an alliance of academics and authors, activists and artists, educators and entrepreneurs who seek to promote simplicity in their work, and seek to practice it in their lives.

ANXIETY CULTURE (UK)

Anxietyculture.com, the brainchild of regular *Idler* contributor Brian Dean, began life as a magazine in 1995. The

website offers a wealth of ideas and gimmicks for navigating "the crazy, paranoid, work-obsessed, media-crapulent times we live in".

CLAWS: CREATING LIVEABLE ALTERNATIVES TO WAGE SLAVERY (USA)

CLAWS calls itself a non-profit pro-leisure and anti-wage slavery support group dedicated to exploring the question, "Why work?" Their main purpose is to "encourage people to value leisure, re-think the Puritan work ethic and its derivatives, and critically examine other work-related legacies of industrial capitalism." CLAWS are not against work per se, but they are critical of the mindset, supported by social norms, government policies and collective fears of poverty, that result in people working against their will and believing there is no other way to "survive". Visit them at Whywork.org.

THE FREE TIME/FREE PEOPLE PROJECT (US)

Founded by a group of big cheeses in various religions and businesses, spearheaded by labour activist and rabbi Art Waskow, their aim is to bring together religious groups, business people, labour leaders, and researchers to reduce work time. Their website (www.shalomctr.org) offers spiritual wisdom, information on work-related government policy, and advice on how to free your time.

TIMESIZING (USA)

Boston's Phil Hyde is the principal researcher of Timesizing.com. The website puts forward a theory of "the best embodiment of worktime economics". The idea is to spread and share the still-un-automated work, the principle being that hours are cut a little for everyone, so that everyone stays employed, instead of jobs being cut completely for a few.

WORK LESS PARTY (CANADA)

"The cycle of produce-consume-produce results in pollution, social decay and forces countries into undesirable competitions and confrontations with one another," say the Work Less Party (worklessparty.org). Their solution is wonderfully simple: Work less. They have organised a number of events, including an annual "Rat Race", in which competitors wearing business attire, whiskers and a tail, run a course and face obstacles, including a power point presentation and a supervisor with managerial aspirations.

WORK TO LIVE (USA)

Joe Robinson's Work to Live website (worktolive.info) shows you "how to beat the unwritten rules of work life, the stuff no one ever talks about that drives overwork, missed vacations, and you to wits end". Robinson, a journalist and editor, has launched the Work to Live Vacation Campaign, which features a petition effort to get a minimum paid-leave law passed in the US.

THE SHORTER WORK-TIME GROUP (SWTGp) (USA)

Founded in 1988 by Women for Economic Justice, this grassroots non-profit project aims to challenge the US's workaholic culture. They provide news about political developments, networking shorter work-time advocates, and bringing the work-time issue into public discussion and the public policy arena. Visit them at swt.org

STORIES

HARRY BRAVADO

A chapter from a novel by
Matthew De Abaitua
Illustrations by Edwin Marney

Monad's office was in a new development in Canary Wharf, the water city out east of Hackney. On the slow approach by robot train, there was plenty of time to admire the skyscraper of One Canada Square, Canary Wharf tower, an obelisk of glass and steel capped with a pyramid. A beacon to capitalism, designed to lure the money men from the City downriver to these reclaimed docklands. Flanked by its vice presidents, the HSBC tower and the Citibank tower, the steel panels of pyramid become alive in the sunlight, the all-seeing eye.

On his first day at work, Raymond felt like he was riding into an office the size of a town. It was hard to tell where the no-smoking zones ended and outdoors began. Getting off at South Quay station, he had a furtive roll-up beside some loading cranes. Two yellow-jacketed security guards gave him a suspicious look, so he re-joined the pedestrian rush-hour on the faux-cobbled walkway. Positioning himself downwind of the shower-fresh hair of three young women, Raymond concentrated on matching everyone else's pace. He was unused to the pace. There were no drags on the course of this river of people; no beggars, no vendors, no tourists, no confused old men, no old women with their trolleys, no madmen berating the pavement. He walked in step with a demographically-engineered London; a hand-picked public uncomplicated by history.

I am finally one of them, thought Raymond. He considered the taste and texture of this thought. Having fought a frankly asymmetrical war against 'them' during his decade in the counter-culture, he expected to feel guilt on the first day of his betrayal.

He didn't.

After walking down Marsh Wall he reached the Meridian bridge, one of two arcing walkways connecting the wharf to the colossal structure that rose out of the water of the West India dock: The Wave Building. Its steel crest sloped down into a trough that ran underwater, only to rise out again a few hundred yards further down the dock: The west wing of The Wave was not only protected by water, it also ran down into the bedrock of the Thames.

The surface of the Wave was smooth burnished steel with no flat planes, offering few impact points for a missile or plunging airliner. Its sinuous steel oscillation bristled with communications antennae; hairs on the back of an immense robotic pachyderm resting in a watering hole. Throughout the lagoon, great ventilation pipes rose out of the water, the sole evidence of the offices buried far beneath. The complex was bound only to the wharf by the filaments of the walkways. These were retractable in the case of alert.

To even get onto the walkway, Raymond had to first pass through a black metal frame, a scanner which chimed softly to signal that he had been analysed, measured, identified and approved.

He tried not to take it as a compliment.

The same PA who had accompanied him on his interview was waiting in the atrium.

"Are you ready to go to work?" she beamed professionally.

He matched her enthusiasm with three quick nods.

He had no idea what he was doing.

He had no idea what his job was.

"My life is a sequence of unusual situations," Raymond explained to me afterwards, his perfect recall sparing me no detail of his first day at work. "I am used to having no idea as to what is going on. This pretty young thing took me down into Monad, asking first date questions along the way. When it was time to leave me, her smile danced across my mind like sunlight upon the Thames. At any other point in the previous ten years, she wouldn't have looked at me. All I could think of was: 'I had no idea that a job would be so handy for getting laid.'"

The orientation exercises took up most of his first week at Monad. To begin with, there was a session watching corporate videos with the other new intake, unsure if he should whisper mocking asides at the blandishments coming from the screen or take notes. Leonard Nimoy and William Shatner presented a short documentary on the "science fiction technology of Monad", in which the aged actors buffooned around with starstruck scientists. "The mind is the final frontier," said Nimoy, striding along a computer-generated replica of the anterior cerebral artery. "Man has postponed his explorations of outer space to journey in here," points to own forehead, "inner space."

"Yes, mind matters!" emphasised Shatner. Both actors had died two years earlier – only a day apart, like an old married couple.

"It's the Laurel And Hardy of Star Trek," whispered Raymond to the woman sitting next to him. It was Florence, and this gag was to play a large role in her decision to sleep with Raymond many months later, outweighing her better judgement. Kirk and Spock's light-hearted links introduced a sequence describing the process by which Monad had licensed a technology from an American company called Dallas Datastream, a technology that allowed them to make a rudimentary simulation of the consciousness of an individual.

"It is impossible to copy someone's soul," said Nimoy, as Shatner was lowered slowly into a cylindrical whole body scanner. "Monad's simulations are like sophisticated reflections in a mirror – they don't have that third dimension that is really you. We record hotspots of molecular activity within crucial areas of the brain through non-invasive surface scanning, combine that with in-depth interviews with the subject, and plug all that information into our model. At the end of it, we get something that looks like you, talks like you, and thinks a bit like you."

The video ended with William Shatner conversing with his simulated self, which – either by vanity or malfunction – looked exactly like the actor at his physical peak. Raymond suspected Shatner would have actually have been dead by the time this recording was made, in which case his estate must have licensed his image for reanimation in this corporate video. An after-life in advertorials.

Disquiet punted itself quietly across his thoughts – Raymond's expression was that of man who had just been told a joke, but is yet to get it.

It was the youthful Shatner that delivered the final earnest speech to

> **All I could think of was: "I had no idea that a job would be so handy for getting laid"**

camera:

"Over the next few days you will encounter concepts and technology that you may find disturbing. If at any time you feel disorientated by Monad, please contact your supervisor immediately."

Raymond was not convinced. He shared his doubt with Florence:

"They can't do that can they? That is impossible, isn't it? Simulating consciousness?"

She shrugged.

"I hate science fiction."

They went for lunch in the Puzzle bar, in the Crossharbour district. There was a provincial quality to Canary Wharf, its sandwich bars (Le Munch Bunch), and Tanning Salons (It's Fast-Tan-Tastic) recalled a light industrial park outside Chester, or a colonnade of shops in an ex-pat enclave in Corfu. Stripped of the diversity and history that characterised London, it was like wandering around a grandiose conference centre.

Lighting a Marlboro, Florence gestured toward the riverside flats. "I used to think how glamourous it would be to live up there. Now I look at the balconies and think how lonely they look, like going into the office on a Sunday."

"A landscape is a state of mind," Raymond observed.

"Is that from Verlaine? Or is it Amiel?"

The discussion turned to poetry. Florence had published a slim volume with Bloodaxe books and had been interning at a small literary magazine before economic necessity had forced her to apply for work at Monad.

"I was appalled when they gave me an interview," she said. "I thought it reflected very badly on me. Obviously they had spied some embarrassing tendency toward conformity in my application."

"We are not exactly Kafka's 'men of business' are we?" said Raymond. He realised he was overdoing the literary references. He was the older man. Florence was only twenty-six. It was unseemly of him to try so hard. He should be silent, like a military man.

Yet he couldn't help rabbiting on. "It is my condition," he apologised, "I get a bit manic when I meet new people."

Florence guided the conversation back to poetry.

"Do you write free verse?"

"Previously. But I have been experimenting with form. The sonnet, the haiku."

"Do you write as quickly as you talk?"

"Yes. Everything all at once. I perform it too, very aggressively."

"I perform like a cat's tail winding around the foot of a bed. Apparently. That's what one critic said about me. I wasn't trying to be sexual but I've got a fantastic pair of tits, and sometimes men take them the wrong way."

From the way Florence was dressed, it was clear she had never had any money. That particular day, there was a Bloomsbury languor to her outfit, which is a polite way of saying she was wearing her dead grandmother's dress. Her blue mac was Chanel, although it had not been dry-cleaned since its previous owner passed away. She did not have the shoulders for its shoulder pads. She wore high heels like an eight-year old boy parading in front of

his mother's bedroom mirror. The second-hand fashion showed an inadvertent eccentricity, a flamboyance that came from an intellectual's carelessness with appearance, rather than a project to mark herself out as an individual.

At this point in his life, Raymond was always immaculate, his figure was that of an Englishman during rationing and so he never wanted for good second hand suits. That day he was wearing a two-button single-breasted blue suit made from a hard-wearing heavy cloth that he boasted "was virtually fire-retardant. Like Kevlar."

Together, they were a charity shop couple, as close as Canary Wharf came to exoticism. Florence even had a ham sandwich stashed in her handbag.

These lunchtime conversations with Florence became part of the routine during the orientation training at Monad. The mornings were spent down in the ambiently-lit lounges of the Wave Building, a timetable of lectures and seminars ("Why The Map Is Not The Territory: Simulation And The Self." and "Against Epiphenomenalism: Your Are Out Of Your Head") during which tides of speculation about the nature of the mind washed over Raymond: silently taking notes, he felt strongly that he knew exactly what the lecturer was on about, and how these profound observations would subsequently alter his view both of himself and reality itself. But as soon as he tried to explain to Florence this insight, his understanding melted away and it was like trying to remember a joke he had heard in a dream. After gasping with astonishment at the revelation that the brain formed second order quantum waves that corresponded to the macroscopic wave functions of outer reality, he forgot it completely. His view

of the world shrugged off these new concepts, they were so counter-intuitive and complex that it was as if his brain was actually resistant to information about itself. He put his forgetting down to the raising of his "reality filters", the screens that protected his vulnerable self against the terrible advance of impossible, unthinkable information.

On Friday afternoon, the entire intake of twenty people was corralled into a meeting room. There wasn't enough chairs for everybody so the men gravitated toward the back, arms crossed and laughing sneering. Eventually Morton Eakins slipped into the room. He was in no hurry to start the meeting. Quietly, as everyone watched him out of the corner of their eye, he unfolded a thin rectangle of transparent, pliable jelly and stuck it on the wall. Slowly the start-up screen appeared, displaying the Monad logo: it looked like a stick man, one central eye, with a semi-circle partially eclipsing the forehead. Once his brain had recovered from the initial anthropomorphizing of the logo, Raymond noticed that it was infact a careful alignment of distinct elements. The head and central cyclopean eye could also be interpreted as the orbit of an electron around a nuclei, or the orbit of a satellite about the Earth. This circle, or head, was set on a cross, which at first glance could be seen as arms and torso, except that the horizontal line bisected the mid-point of the vertical, contrary to the traditional stick man, whose arms are drawn slanting downwards from the neck. Either side of the base of the cross, there was a quarter-circle, which joined together like a child's scrawl of an arse or, other way around, tits. In fact it looked like this:

The logo had more lines than the standard brand, and was more like a glyph or sigil.

Eakins pointed to the figure:

"This is Monad."

He exhaled, an evangelist's awe at the revelation he was about to impart.

"What is it?"

Some of the intake went to answer, but Eakins moved on.

"Monad is a mystery."

On the screen, the Monad logo morphed into a question mark.

"Why has Monad employed you? What does Monad want you to do? Where did Monad come from and where is it going? This past week, we have laid on a crash-course in philosophies of the self, the latest research into consciousness, the structure of the brain, and the implications of artificial intelligence. But we have not answered the big question: what you are doing here?"

Eakins' hairline was retreating.

Unfortunate deposits of fat gave him dugs and a slight gullet that bowed beneath his chin. There was a hairless, beardless babyish quality to Eakins: his black company fleece and black moleskin trousers resembled a funereal romper suit. He wore a thick gold band wedding ring, had once had his ears pierced, and his skull erred toward the oblong. There was a weak and soft quality to his physiognomy that aroused an instinctive hatred in Raymond.

Certainly Eakins wasn't a genetic catch.

On his desk, there was a picture of his wife on their wedding day.

It wasn't a close-up.

Eakins also liked the sound of his own voice.

"What if your consciousness could be uploaded into a computer? It's a common idea in science fiction. It proceeds from the assumption that the mind, like the computer, is a consequence of computation. You are merely a collection of neurons firing in network, therefore it is a simply a matter of recording the position of those neurons and mapping those locations onto a model that interprets them as thoughts, memories, the qualia that is the ineffable You.

"Over the last five days, we have raised these kind of speculations and hopefully you have realized that is impossible to upload your mind into a computer, using current technology.

"We could analyse your entire brain. Peel it like an onion and record the constituency of each slice of tissue with an electron microscope. It would kill you, and to what purpose? In every cubic millimeter of brain matter there are ten to the power of five neurons and ten to the power of nine synapses. That is before we even get onto the nervous system. Or the multitude of chemical and hormonal activity that composes you. How would we reassemble this map of your brain into a mind? Where would we get the model from that could run that program? What computer could possibly contain such an immensity of information?

"You could take a baby, I suppose. A tabula rasa. Expose them to carefully controlled stimuli while constantly recording the development of brain. Show them their mother's face, note down the concomitant swell of neural activity.

Perhaps the baby would wear a magnetic resonance helmet that could map the growth of their consciousness every day for the first five years of their life. Would that give you the information you needed to reconstruct a consciousness from a brain scan?

"Then there are broader philosophical problems. Consciousness can be seen as an evolutionary adaptation, a survival mechanism that has allowed our species to flourish. As such it is not merely housed in the body, but it innately bound up with sensory perception and the proprioceptions – your sense of the space you occupy. Mind may not exist without body. Lightening is a phenomenon of weather, and once it is separated from the system within which it arises, it ceases to be lightening, and is merely a spark.

"It is vital that you understand the distinction between simulated and uploaded consciousness. Why? Monad simulates its customers, and you are going to be explaining to those customers precisely what has happened to them. There must be no misapprehension that the simulation is a perfect copy of them, or that it constitutes some form of immortality. The reason why I employed you is because you are all writers, mainly poets. You have the rare conceptual elasticity to simplify this mind-boggling

"Consciousness can be seen as an evolutionary adaptation"

situation, and you will need to do that on a daily basis as you field calls and complaints from our client base."

The Monad brand appeared again on the screen.

The Horned devil with cloven hoof. Taurus. Even the cuckold. On closer inspection: a modulation of the symbols of Mars and Venus to mark a third sex, a new species.

"Any questions?" asked Eakins.

Florence raised her hand.

"Assembling a menagerie of poets to deal with some weird hypothetical technology seems to me - and I don't want you to take this the wrong way - I mean, I appreciate the money and everything - but this is madness."

Eakins indulged her with a smirk.

"There is a call centre in Italy that employs only actors. Actors always need money, and are gifted improvisers. Therefore a call centre staffed by actors is more appropriate for certain products, specifically those that don't lend

themselves to a scripted approach. I don't think there has ever been a poet customer service department before. It was my idea. Poetry attracts psychological types we think will be the best fit as a liaison between a client and their simulant.

Since the money you earn will support your art, we would expect a lower staff turnover. Also, being poets, you're very cheap."

Eakins laughed like a man who had no

"The future always seems strange at first"

taste for humour.

Raymond had a question.

"When do we meet a simulated person?"

"Now," said Eakins.

On the screen, the Monad symbol dissolved and after a brief loading screen, millions of pixels flared and resolved into an image of an open-plan living room, late afternoon sun streaming in through the large windows of the west wall. The rays of light with their whirling motes struck a false note, a cinematographer's self-indulgence. Raymond also noted the impossibility in the way their viewpoint rose and tracked across the room. The velocity of their progress suggested the environment was rotating about their position, with the camera as fixed axis rather than roaming eye.

With a sudden giddy realignment, like the spin of a compass needle returning to magnetic north, the view veered about to fix upon a doorway.

A man stepped through. He was fastening his cuff-links, then threading his tie through a starched white collar.

"Good morning Eakins. Who do you have for me today?" Now they got a close look at him. He was ugly, insofar as his features were exaggerated, a shelf of thickly-haired brow and pores so open they suggested foam packaging rather than flesh. Simian lips curling into a smile, the algebra of which was complex with self-satisfaction and contempt. He shrugged into his suit jacket and lounged on a black leather armchair, his crotch pushed forward.

Raymond and his fellow employees stared with disbelief. When they realised that this unreal apparition was scrutinising them in turn, they shifted to expressions of horror and awe.

"I can spare five of your Earth minutes," said the hypothetical man, removing a cigarette from a gold case. He had a novelty lighter in the shape of a nude woman. "Shoot."

Florence raised her hand and the unreal man nodded to her.

She said: "Who are you?"

"I am Unit four five slash oh one six point eight." A bark of laughter followed by an exhalation of nicotine pleasure. "Sorry that's an old Monad joke. Seriously. My name used to be Harold Blasebalk, but now I call myself Harry Bravado. It makes things easier."

"But do you know what you are?"

"You mean, do I have any issues with the fact that I am simulated person? No. Knowing you are unreal is nowhere near as distressing as realising you are mortal. Anyway, who are you?"

Florence looked at Raymond to confirm that he was as unsettled as she was. He could manage only a wide-eyed shrug.

"My name's Florence."

"What's your number, Florence?" Again, Harry Bravado laughed at his own joke, adjusted the leg of his trousers. The suggestion of a hefty cock and balls showed against his thigh.

Raising his hand to intervene, Eakins moved to the front of the auditorium. Silhouetted against Bravado's immense leer, he explained the history of this particular simulated individual. The real Harold Blasebalk was a new business manager for one of Monad's suppliers.

After a course of rigorous interviews and observations of his behaviour, Blasebalk's brain was scanned and maps were constructed of its molecules and atoms – not a complete picture, not the whole man, but "good enough". Out of these two studies, the Blasebalk simulation was hypothesised. It went conscious five months earlier and quickly insisted on being known as Harry Bravado, a decision that could be read either as an indication that it was not an accurate simulation, or that it had chosen to become Blasebalk's idealised version of his own self.

Raymond interrupted:

"What does the real Harry Blasebalk think of you?"

Bravado finished his cigarette.

"Since I was uploaded into Monad, I have helped him secure 2 million dollars in new billings.

That's no mean feat considering the economic conditions out there. He takes a percentage of gross fees so his basic take home is triple his previous salary. So I'd imagine he's pretty fucking pleased with himself."

"How do you help him?"

"Analysis of opportunities. Close observation of competitors. Every notion he has, he sends me an email and I follow it through. I am both his very personal assistant and, simultaneously, his boss."

Raymond laughed. "Why does he still bother going to work?"

"My continuing existence depends upon it," the simulated man did not appreciate Raymond's smile. "If Blasebalk gets fired, they will probably switch me off. The executive who replaced him would want his own simulation. His own Me2."

"Is that what you are? A Me2?"

"It's what they call us. Me2 is our name and our core proposition. Me2 is our genus and our brand."

A soft low chime sounded in the penthouse. Bravado made one last pass at straightening his tie while Eakins thanked for him for his time.

As the screen dimmed, the lights in the auditorium came up. Eakins returned to the podium and faced an audience of people, some of whom were laughing with the rising hysteria of shock.

"To begin with, we will be limiting your interaction with the Me2s. What you have just seen is not as mind-blowing as it first appears. This really is nothing other than cutting edge ventriloquism. If any of you are inclined to anxiety or panic, remember splashing your face with cold water will slow your pulse and help you regain some equilibrium. This is the end of your first week of induction. Have a good weekend and we will resume first thing Monday."

Eakins strode from the auditorium. Ushers appeared and led the audience of poets out to the large elevators. They rose up from the secure underwater section of The Wave building to a large atrium, a geodesic tessellation of panes looking out over the Thames. A small buffet was laid out on a table, and there were staff serving glasses of wine. A light rain falling in Morse code against the glass, a dot a dash a dot dot dash. Raymond scooted past the plates of food, and secured a drink for himself and for Florence. The woman was at a railing staring out at the water city.

"Tomorrow this will all be part of our normality," she said. She took the glass of wine and glugged it back greedily.

"The future always seems strange, at first," said Raymond. He could see that she had been crying and so he put his arm around her. She shrugged it off, then thought better of it. ◉

THE APPLICATION

A short story by Clare Pollard
Illustrations by Marcus Oakley

1) Please give details of work experience, both paid and unpaid:
Before last month, I was a very different person. For a start, I never had a sense of vocation. Other girls wanted to be air hostesses, vets, TV presenters, footballer's wives – but I just drifted towards my future, trying not to dwell on it. I do remember my mother, once, suggested teaching good holidays). Soon afterwards, when I mooted this with my father, who I'd meet at weekends for trips to expensive, frigid restaurants or educational hands-on museums, he told me quite forcibly that the children of tomorrow were "clinically obese scum," and suggested law (good pay.) In the end, I took biological sciences at university because it was my best subject. Well, that or geography.

And then stuff just happened. I met Rory in my last year at university, started temping afterwards whilst I found a proper job, and found it slowly became permanent. Filing, franking, faxing, typing forgettable things into the computer. The only thing I enjoyed about it was the nice sandwich bar on the corner where I always got lunch: a skinny latte and a Mexican three-bean wrap, or else a chicken caesar salad bowl. I always got one or the other. Also I liked shopping for work clothes on my lunch breaks: corsages, capes – the kind of stuff that goes out of fashion within the fortnight. At the weekend I just flopped around in jeans.

2) Please give details of why you have applied for the post of telephone psychic and why you would like to work for Psychic Gift:
We drove down the narrow lane towards my father's cottage, which we were borrowing for another weekend. Rory always drove. I sat beside him, my window down, chill-out music blaring out. "Chewing gum?" I asked.

"No. No thanks." In the boot we had a chicken, a bag of spuds, carrots, cabbage and gravy powder. I was going to make a proper Sunday roast that night, for John and his girlfriend – Salina? Selena? – with a few glasses of the New World wine that had been on offer at Tesco. We would sit in the garden, by the stream where tiny frogs sometimes hopped, intricate as origami. I'd burn mosquito coils.

"I wish we had some weed," I said, although I was indifferent really, but knew Rory usually liked some, and wanted to make conversation.

"Uh-huh," he replied. It annoyed me sometimes. All the little things I did to please him, to make our relationship work – all the talking about his career, and pretending to have an interest in Italian football, and faking it – and he didn't even know. It seemed like it was only me who made an effort.

"Maybe John'll have some," I suggested.

"Yep, maybe."

"I'm really looking forward to relaxing," I added. I'd worked overtime all week. Really, I'd have preferred it if John hadn't been coming, as I always found socialising a drag at the weekend. When I was tired I just liked to vote people out of reality shows. If I'd said anything though, Rory would just have gone into one of his moods: he's my best friend, you're so selfish, blah blah blah. We hadn't met this girlfriend before. She was American, apparently – John had met her whilst he was doing work experience in New York – and I was secretly expecting her to be loud and ill-informed and on the Atkins diet. Salina? Selena? The gum had turned blank in my mouth. "What do you think she'll be like?" I asked.

"She sounded a bit of an annoying bitch to me," he replied. His even, handsome face was slightly blotchy, his tan hair at careless angles. He'd had a pill the night before, and I reassured myself that this was why he seemed down. Placed my hand on his knee. A sheep, the colour of curdled milk, ambled past.

When we got to the cottage, the boiler wasn't working.

A crow crooked its head on the gatepost.

Four hours later we were all in the garden, with its sycamore, its stream, the sagging white roses by the fence – small, moth-eaten wedding dresses. I had laid out the table with ivory candles and my dad's serving dishes piled with veg. "Christ, Karen's been body-snatched by Delia Smith," John joked, and I didn't think it was a nice joke, and was disappointed that Rory said nothing. Rory looked good that night, in a pink shirt, which he'd read in one of the Sundays was a hot colour for men.

"Enjoying England, yeah?" he asked

Selena, as she pulled out her chair to sit down. She smiled a generous smile.

"Why thank you! Yes I am. It's a funny time right now though, you know. I almost cancelled the flight."

"It must be super-safe though," John declared. "You can't even have plastic forks. What are they going to hijack the plane with – a complimentary eye-mask? A very small cup of coffee?"

"I guess it's just… something like that happens and you never feel the same again."

"Here you are," I said, heaping protein on people's plates. "There's gravy in the boat." I always felt boring around John: he was a raconteur, the life-and-soul. Then I realised Selena was staring at me with her clever, brown eyes.

"I have a thing about people you know," she declared, leaning towards me. Pushing her beautiful hair, the colour of burnt-sugar, from her cheek. "I do auras. You have a very special aura." Wind shivered through the rhododendron bush, and prickled our bare arms to gooseflesh. I laughed.

"Yeah, right."

"I think you have a spiritual side, no really, I do. I'm gonna get out my cards later and –"

"Not again," John said.

"Yes, again," Selena said, and turned to me and smiled. I liked her.

3) Please give details of relevant qualifications and training:
The clock on the microwave said: 1:43.

Since we had moved the stuff inside because of stormy looking clouds, Selena had held a séance that didn't work – she blamed "a, like, total lack of seriousness" – and read all our tarot cards, and predicted lots of vague life-changing experiences. We were all pretty stoned,

and pissed on the elderflower and gooseberry wine we'd got round the corner off some locals. John had since imitated their "yokel accents" whilst pretending to fuck a cow, and everyone had laughed, especially Rory.

I wasn't as pissed as the others as I always hold back a bit, and not as stoned either as I can't inhale very well – have always been too timid about taking it down into my lungs – but I was still pretty gone, basically, and was trying unconvincingly to find the other bottle of red in the kitchen, amongst the raggedy chicken bones, the gravy congealing to soft glass, the blaze of unwanted carrots. I thought the bottle was still in a supermarket bag. Wasn't it in the fridge? "Rory?" I shouted. "Wasen it in the fredge, fridge?"

"Dunno," he answered, and then I heard him giggling again at something John had said.

"I thought it was."

"I said I don't know."

I found it, suddenly, right in front of me beside the mayo as though it had been magicked there, and felt silly. "Salright, son the cupboard," I lied. It had begun to rain, as expected, transparent rosaries flicking against the windows.

"Hey," Selena yelled from the living room. "Lets do this psychic thing right, I did it the other night and it so worked. It was awesome."

I opened the bottle with some effort, and filled up my glass. I moved through to the lounge, where the men had put on some of my dad's vinyl, a Bowie record, I think. I've never paid much attention to music. John's glass had left a ring on the biscuit-coloured carpet, and I felt annoyed that he was just sat there, staring at it, when it wasn't even my carpet but my dad's. "No more new age bullshit please," he said.

"I'll have a go," I told Selena, and Rory looked up surprised. I don't know why I said it. Maybe it was that thing Selena said about auras. "It's interesting," I added.

"Yes," Selena beamed. "It is, isn't it?"

"More wine," John demanded, and she passed him the bottle. He slopped some in his glass messily. Rory was rolling a joint. He's good at rolling, deft.

Selena patted the rug beside me, and I sat on it. "Okay, I'm going to try and read your mind, okay?" She said. "I did it last week, at this party, right? I got like nine out of ten people's numbers right, they were so spooked. But it's not creepy or anything, it's just about harnessing those parts of the brain that we don't usually utilise. Now – imagine a black board, and a number on it in white. Concentrate."

I imagined a seven.

"Five, right?"

"No," I said, vaguely disappointed. John laughed.

"Nine?"

"Nope."

"Shit, I had this last week." Selena drained her wine. The rain picked up, filling the small, timbered room with noise. The candlelight made her face wobbly. "Well, maybe I'm not getting the vibe. You try."

4) Please give details of your experience related to this post and skills you have to offer:
I closed my eyes and tried very hard to imagine a dark, black space. I waited for a number to come. Slowly, as if shaped by an invisible hand, a white numeral emerged against the void. "Okay, erm." I felt stupid. John was watching me hotly. Rory tried to stop himself smirking pre-emptively, and wait for the moment he

could share it with his friend. "Ssss-six," I managed. Selena did a tiny jump of glee.

"Woah, yeah! Six! It was six!"

"Bull," John said, moving over to her and pushing a dry little kiss onto her forehead. "You're bullshitting us darling."

"Okay, mister smart-ass, try it," Selena said. "Write it down." Rory lit the joint and took his first, deep lungful. "Right!" Selena yelled, when she'd found a biro. "Now, come on John."

He wrote a number down on a scrap of receipt, sheltering it with his cupped hand.

I closed my eyes and re-imagined the dark, black space. I waited for a number to come, and it did, the hand shaping it again – a 43, ha-ha, very funny, and then, more, it kept coming – I.... h a t e.... I opened my eyes, and looked into his eyes, suddenly sickened, and looked down into my wine, and saw the letters spell out on the purplish red. I hate myself.

"Forty three," I said softly, and John's face turned to candle wax.

"Fuck!" he declared, after seven, eight seconds. "No way! You two are coding or something, you worked it out in the kitchen, right?"

We shook our heads. Selena passed me the joint. "Hey, whoah. I've only seen that work from one to ten."

My hands were shaking. I dropped ash on my leg, took a weak suck, passed the joint hastily on.

5) *Please add anything about yourself that you feel is relevant in support of your application*

In the bathroom I splashed my face. Dark petals of wine were glued to my lips, and the red rimmed my teeth. A mosquito quivered around the light bulb. I squeezed some soap onto my hands and washed them, and all the while I could

hear John and Rory chatting, and Selena's voice, like a low constant murmur behind it.

I think you're a loser.

I pity you.

It was my mind playing tricks, wasn't it? It had to be. You are NOT reading her mind, I told my reflection sternly. And anyway, why would she pity me? I was fine, wasn't I? I didn't have the career of my dreams, okay – but I had this house at the weekends, quite nice clothes, a good-looking boyfriend... Still I heard her whisper.

I just wanted to involve you in tonight.

You seemed so left out.

I pity you.

I went back into the lounge. "Rory's going to do it now, aren't you Rory?" Selena said. I could see that she had already given him a pen and paper. He looked down at them, his eyes hidden from mine beneath their hooded lids.

"Oh, it's. It's nonsense, I guess, just lucky," I told them, feigning interest in the bookcase. I picked up my glass again, and topped it up with more wine. Took a slurp, wanting to get drunker: for everything to get more radiant and shaky and unreal. Rory looked up at me, and it seemed, somehow, like he was grateful.

I was used to pleasing him. "Let's leave it for now," I added. " Change the record. I'm sick of this old stuff."

"No, no, you have to!" Selena implored. "Have you any idea how, like, amazing that was?"

"Go on," John agreed.

The number was 118.

I won't tell you what else I read.

I threw the glass against the wall, and it smashed and bled.

Selena said: "You've got it, haven't you?" ❧

THE PRACTICAL
IDLER

THE PRACTICAL IDLER

Welcome to the Practical Idler. In this issue we've got Dan Kieran's guide to what to do about the money problem when seeking the idle life. Elsewhere we celebrate the pleasures of fishing, fencing, taking tea, taking notes, building your own sauna, smoking cigars and driving a Vauxhall Corsa. We take a look at writer Geoff Dyer's bookshelf and visit the Freedom Bookshop in London, E1. And we meet the maverick DJ Unfit For Work while Julian Watson provides an insight into the laid back attitude of Cambodians when it comes to work. So, lots of good things, lots of good thoughts.

YOUR GUIDE TO THE EASY LIFE

171 **Seven Steps To The Idle Life:** Dan Kieran counsels wisdom

176 **The Angler:** Kevin Parr is on the river bank

179 **Notebook Of The Month:** The very splendid Moleskine

180 **WD40:** Chris Yates recommends the wonderstuff

182 **Fencing:** We meet a master of the art

184 **Saunas:** Will Hogan knows how to build your own hot house

186 **Tea Time:** Chris Yates has a cure for melancholy

188 **The Passenger:** Fanny Johnstone is comforted by the Vauxhall Corsa

190 **Cigars:** Tim Richardson befuddles himself with smoke

194 **The Browser:** Geoff Dyer's bookshelf; Steve Aylett on Jeff Lint, and a trip to the Freedom Bookshop

200 **Easy Sounds:** DJ Unfit For Work is mad for it and John Moore reveals the arts of independent record production

206 **The Idler Abroad:** Julian Watson is in Cambodia

211 **Film:** Paul Hamilton on Marlon Brando's lazy phase

220 **Back Issues**

224 **Greg Rowland's View From The Sofa**

IDLE PURSUITS:
SEVEN STEPS TO THE IDLE LIFE

Can't afford to be an idler? Think again. By Dan Kieran
Illustrations by Foreign Office

As a dedicated man of the sloth I am always putting forward the merits of an idler life to anyone who will listen. But whether it's in the pub, on late radio night phone-ins or dodgy cable TV shows, the response is always the same: "Well, it's all right for you to be an Idler but the rest of us can't afford it. Some of us have to work for a living."

This argument will resonate with some but it's important to point out that the *Idler* isn't a network of smug, independently wealthy parasites. There's nothing unusual about any of us, but we all do have one thing in common. At some time or other, we've all taken a leap into the unknown to pursue a different kind of life. So if you can't face spending another day doing a pointless job that you hate; if you loath the fact that you only get four weeks a year to actually "live" and spend the other forty-eight staring at a clock, wishing your life away; if you want a different, more idle life and you don't know how to get one, or don't think you can afford one, here's a seven-step guide.

STEP ONE – GIVE UP EVER WANTING TO BE RICH
In the words of that apostle of the amateur creed, poet/painter/musician Billy Childish: "If they've got what you want then they've got you." So if you can stop wanting what they've got then you've already cracked the hardest part of becoming an Idler and a life of freedom is yours for the taking. Not wanting to be rich is the single most immediate and liberating act you will ever make in your life. Of course some Idlers become rich accidentally as a result of following their natural instincts, but being rich is never their goal, just a stone that gets into their shoe somewhere along the journey.

STEP TWO – RID YOURSELF OF DEBT

Mortgage, literally translated, means "death grip" – such is the patronising and bloated nature of the lender/borrower relationship.

But western society is built on foundations of overwork and over-consumption so a life without debt is becoming increasingly difficult to attain. The mortgage is probably the only type of debt we can no longer live without and still remain self-sufficient but all other kinds of debt are completely avoidable.

The cycle of debt is what traps most people in a job and a life they hate. The harder they work the more miserable and stressed they become.

So they go to the shops at the weekend and buy themselves something nice because they've had a tough week. Even if they don't have enough money they can still buy whatever they want with a criminally usurious credit or store card. But when their statement appears they get that gnawing feeling of dread in the middle of their stomachs as they realise the mountain their debt has become. So they work even harder, they take all the over-time they can get to pay for everything they've bought to make them less stressed, which makes them even more miserable.

They work so hard, in fact, that the rest of the time they're totally exhausted, they're either arguing with the person they love, becoming strangers to their children or drowning their sorrows in the pub. And by this point, because they're in so much debt, they can't live a different life even if they wanted to. Those spiralling monthly payments have trapped them in a crap job in a crap house that's full of crap that they don't need.

Ridding yourself of debt will give you the opportunity to live a different kind of life but it can take time, years even, to clear. Bear in mind though that even if it takes you ten years this is a much more sensible thing to pursue than a career.

STEP THREE - DON'T BUY USELESS CRAP THAT YOU DON'T NEED

Everyone buys useless crap that they don't need and don't use to compensate for the misery of their forty-eight week a year job that destroys their soul and dignity. Take responsibility for your own happiness and stop trying to fill the hole in your life with grot. This doesn't mean wearing rags, growing a beard and patronising anyone who wears Nike trainers.

Just bear in mind that the more you buy, the more you'll have to work to pay for it. Remember the rule is no credit. So if you can't afford it you can't have it.

STEP FOUR – DITCH YOUR PENSION

The pension is one of society's so-called safety nets that doesn't actually make any of us feel safe. Pensions and retirement itself form the carrot that goes with the stick of work to create what *Idler* Editor at Large Matthew De Abaitua calls "the secular afterlife". "Work hard, be miserable now and save just enough money so you can stay alive in penury when you're old and grey," say those who advocate pensions. Er, no thanks. But this is the life and the fate that awaits those of us who've helped make the UK the fourth largest economy in the world. (What was the point of that then? Where's all the money gone?) Pensions aren't safe. Invest your money in yourself and your own happiness now instead of a pension plan that will probably vanish sometime in the future.

Pensions are also the justification for corporate greed as Chief Executives bleat about "the needs of shareholders" to justify their savage pursuit of a rising share value. Nothing is allowed to get in the way of increasing a company's share price. Whether it's decimating any sense of community in our towns and villages across the country by building gross, unnecessary warehouse style shopping malls, closing village banks or selling arms to dictators. So if you want to do your bit for the planet remove any money you have from the stock exchange. This simple act will improve your life and, indirectly, the lives of other Idlers all over the

world.

STEP FIVE – WORK PART-TIME

Once you've given up wanting to be rich, you've got yourself out of debt and you've stopped buying crap that you don't need you'll find that you need much less money to live on than before. So now you can quit your full-time job and get a part-

on a Tuesday. Otherwise visit our chat board at www.idler.co.uk.)

If going part-time is a daunting prospect then work four days a week to start with and gradually wean yourself off your addiction to work. A three-day a week job is popular with many Idlers now, four days off, three days on is a far more civilised way of living than the criminal two days off, five days on, that our greedy western world depends on.

STEP SIX – DO THAT THING YOU'VE ALWAYS DREAMT OF DOING

Once you've worked through the guilt of not being "a productive member of society" (i.e. you've stopped working and consuming more than you need in order to be happy), you'll find time on your hands to pursue the things you've always wanted to do. Far from being an unrealistic goal this is precisely where your future security actually lies.

The Idler's ultimate goal is to earn a living doing something so enjoyable that it can scarcely be called work at all. And when the way you earn a living is something you love doing then the idea of retirement becomes ludicrous, so you won't need a pension either.

It will take time, but eventually you will work out how to earn money doing

time one instead.

Part-time jobs are more and more popular with businesses because they remove a company's legal obligation to give you the benefits associated with full-time work, sick pay and so on. But that's OK because the happier you are the healthier you are and the less you work the happier you will become so you won't need these so called benefits.

At this point, as you while away the hours reading and sunbathing in the park, you may find yourself feeling guilty that you don't have a full time job. This is hardly surprising. Since primary school you have been brainwashed into thinking that hard work is virtuous. Well, it bloody well isn't. As the late Jeffrey Bernard once said: "If there was anything virtuous about hard work the Duke of Westminster would dig his own fucking garden, wouldn't he?" Ignore the guilt, enjoy your new spare time, have a lie in and if you start feeling that you're no longer a productive member of society then ring the Idler office on 0207 691 0320 and we'll talk you though your panic attack. (Although we'll only be in the office whatever it is you want to do with your life. Later you will earn enough to cut down the hours of your part-time job until eventually you'll be able to quit the world of the crap job completely.

This is the Idler's life. Seeking happiness, not success, and wisdom rather than cleverness. As *Idler* fan and TV supremo John Lloyd puts it: "people are obsessed with cleverness when it's wisdom that counts, and anyone can be wise. It's also impossible to be wise and not be good." Or as freedom-seeker Peter Doherty wrote: "I'm so clever, but clever ain't wise." With wisdom comes the acceptance of truth, personal happiness and the creative, self-directed life so many of us crave.

STEP SEVEN – TAKE THE TEST

Read this passage. If you can read it without shuddering then you've made it, if you can't there's still time, there's always time.

Old bureaucrat, my companion here present, no man ever opened an escape route for you, and you are not to blame. You built peace for yourself by blocking up every chink of light, as termites do. You rolled yourself into your ball of bourgeois security, your routines, the stifling rituals of your provincial existence; you built your humble rampart against winds, tides and stars. You have no wish to ponder great questions; you had enough trouble suppressing awareness of your human condition. You do not dwell on a wandering planet, you ask yourself no unanswerable questions; ...No man ever grasped you by the shoulder while there was still time.

> The Idler's ultimate goal is to earn a living doing something so enjoyable that it can scarcely be called work at all

Now the clay that formed you has dried and hardened, and no man could now awaken in you the dormant musician, the poet or the astronomer who perhaps once dwelt within you.

From *Wind, Sand and Stars* by Antoine de Saint-Exupéry.

THE ANGLER:
BRING ME MY ROD

Kevin Parr arms himself with his fishing rod in the War against Work. Illustration by Joe Harrison

Arthur Aplin, author of *The Philandering Angler*, was distraught one day in Brittany. The morning looked promising – crisp air, warm sunshine, a lovely day to perform his art. And, yet, the hotel manager seemed determined that he should leave – for good.

"No," argued Aplin, somewhat perplexed. "I will be back for dinner with a plateful of trout."

He was one of the hotel's most valued customers. He paid well, he was polite, courteous, and, though on occasion the maid may have spent longer in his chamber than professional duties decreed, he held his host with respect.

Suddenly, though, they wanted him out, and what was more, the staff were actually packing up and leaving themselves. "One more day, at least grant me that," Aplin pleaded. "Sir," came the reply, "we are at war. Within days your river will be bombed and the town overrun with German soldiers – you must leave."

Such is the mind of an angler, and though Aplin's complete disregard for current affairs is somewhat extreme, no singular sober activity takes your mind so far away from the everyday grind as fishing. Alas, from mid-March the angler must be content to read about his preferred past-time in books. But mid-June heralds both the start of the fishing season, and also the longest days of the year. Such perfect coincidences should always be exploited.

My school bus used to chug past my favourite pond, and I would always seat myself carefully to give an optimum view of my favourite swim. The close season, from mid-March to mid-June, would offer daily changes on the pond, and as the lilies spread and the water colour deepened, so my excitement would intensify. By the time the season arrived I would be fit to burst, and on the night of the fifteenth, season's eve, I wouldn't sleep a wink. Instead I would rise before dawn, jump on my bicycle and pedal my way in the emerging light in order to make my first cast. I knew the pond well, and would invariably catch at least one tench, before the sun poked over the reed-beds and I had to dash for home. Amazingly, I always made it back in time for the school bus and I would retrace my journey of just a few hours before with a glorious sense of surreal satisfaction.

Throughout the ensuing school day, I would then be invincible. I was safe from tetchy teachers and marauding bullies, comfortably cocooned in the memory of my stolen dawn's fishing.

Education, like work, is a continual thorn in the fisherman's side. Fortunately my pond was a mere twenty-minute bike ride away, though passing my driving test at seventeen was a revelation. Suddenly, a spare hour could equate to forty minutes on the bank, and I could get to know my water with greater intimacy.

Sadly, though, the membership of Alresford Angling Club had dwindled to four and as a result was ceasing to be. I had one last season to crack the place.

It was an unforgiving venue, holding few fish, which were wild and wily. Though I had achieved success with most species, I was determined to make a big catch of roach, of which there were very few, but very large. Throughout that final season, I focussed all my angling attention upon a shoal of maybe a dozen fish. Roach that were possibly as old as I, and certainly more streetwise.

Come February and I'd got them almost sussed. I knew precisely where they lived, at what depth they would feed, and which bait they were most partial to. I had also determined their favourite feeding time – an hour or so before dusk. All I needed now was perfect weather conditions.

It was a week before the end of the season when I found myself in A-Level Film Studies, gazing out of the window at the mild overcast sky, when I realised that now was the time. I considered that I had around two and a half hours to drive thirty miles to the pond, picking up a rod from home on the way, and get back to collect my mother from work (it was her car, after all). That left a little over an hour and a quarter on the bank, and a good excuse needed for missing photography.

Time smiled so sweetly, though, and that stolen angle seemed to last forever. My intuition was rewarded by a catch of ten roach over a pound and a quarter, including two of two pounds. More fish than I had caught all season, and on my last ever trip to the pond.

Though this proved to me just how obliging time and luck will be if you break the routine of work or education, it was further demonstrated some years later after a Sunday night phone call from Kieran.

Kieran was fed up, and he never gets fed up, yet city life and the daily grind had worn him bare. "Come fishing," I suggested. Living in Doleland had given me a sensibly straightforward attitude to life's problems. "Maybe," Kieran mused, and he did.

I took him down to the Hampshire Avon, which in mid-July provided the perfect contrast from London life. Within minutes of reaching the top meadow, Kieran had unwound. "I don't feel the need to fish..." he said, and with the sun rising and buzzards wheeling overhead, I couldn't disagree.

All we caught until mid-afternoon were grasshoppers and the sun, but, with a summer storm billowing, I felt a need to provide Kieran with his first fish.

We found a shoal of wily chub about a mile downstream, and with the evening drawing, attempted everything to catch one. These were very bright fish, though, and were not to be easily fooled. Time was running out when suddenly Kieran's rod hooped over. I dashed down the bank to help but the chub was already being bullied into the net.

And what a chub!

Kieran's first proper fish (trout don't count) and a specimen of five pounds seven ounces. I was unashamedly green with envy.

And as we ventured home, my friend slumped low, smiling and contented in the passenger seat, we reflected upon the fortune of the day, and the ease with which he could return to work, refreshed if not wholly cured.

"Life ain't so bad," I thought to myself, and when the war against work truly begins, then stick me in the front line, for I shall be armed with a fishing rod. 🐟

STATIONARY REVIEW:

THE MOLESKINE

Value you thoughts, jot them down in a notebook
By Tom Hodgkinson

DIARIES AVAILABLE AT www.bureau-online.co.uk

A notebook is a crucial piece of weaponry in the war against work. Instead of befuddling your poor mind with advertising and newspapers as you go about your daily business, it is sensible to keep a notebook in your pocket to record your daydreams, thoughts and ideas. A notebook is an essential tool if you want to be something more than a work-robot, an efficiency machine. Abandon the empty promises of digital organisers and embrace the creativity and anarchy of pen and paper. You may feel a trifle self-conscious when you first get the notebook out. You may worry that people around you on the bus will think you have got ideas above your station. You may think that the very act of jotting down thoughts in a book implies a sort of arrogance, that you consider your thoughts to be worth jotting down in the first place. Ignore these negative emotions, which have been produced in your mind by years of conditioning by the industrial society, conditioning that says only the experts have got anything to say. Most great ideas come from notebooks: when Wordsworth and Coleridge wrote Lyrical Ballads, it didn't just pour from their pens spontaneously. It was the result of wild wanderings and jottings, later tamed into poetic form. Dylan Thomas sought material in the pub: he would sit in the corner, writing down snippets of the conversation he heard around him, in order to understand the rhythms of everyday speech. With your notebook, you will elevate yourself to the status of poet, writer and entrepreneur. Value your mind and its contents.

And this month's featured notebook is the classic Moleskine, famously beloved of Bruce Chatwin who created his writing out of their raw material he recorded in his Moleskines. They are made in Italy, they are hardback and feature a page marker and a useful pocket at the back, where tickets and ephemera can be stored.

Some notebook lovers find the Moleskine a tad on the stiff side – they will not bend to the contours of a back pocket – but that is the only objection we can find to these beautiful friends of every idler. ◉

SURVIVAL KIT:

SPRAY YOUR CHORES AWAY

Chris Yates on why WD40 should be the first item on your shopping list. Illustration By Will Yates

I was interested to hear on the news last week that police drug squads have been recommending the use of WD40 at "problem" clubs and pubs. Apparently, managers have been advised to apply the wonder spray to those areas where white dust is regularly snorted. Anyone who subsequently sprinkles a line of gak will see it transformed into a kind of paraffin and vegetable oil mash as it absorbs the WD. I shall have to remember this, as it would be terrible to risk spoiling my own drug of choice – tea – though a careless blast of WD in the kitchen. And there is always a can handy in the kitchen. Recently, the electric kettle stopped working. I looked at the wiring and it was intact. I checked the fuse: ok. I dabbed at the fittings with a tissue to remove any moisture. I switched the kettle on again: nothing. And it was that time, around 4pm, when the whole universe pauses like a shambling procession coming to a suddenly abrupt halt – because nothing further can happen until the tea-time tea is made and imbibed.

What could I do? Soon it would be ten past the hour and the world would collapse without its proper punctuation.

But wait! I didn't need to turn out the camping stove because next to the washing up liquid and the floor cleaner was the can of WD40. A quick blast of spray into the electric's, a careful refilling with water; switch it on, and ah! That reassuring hiss of a functioning heating element. The kettle has never given me any grief again.

Besides electrical maintenance and drug prevention WD also makes a spectacular fire starter. My sole source of heating in this house is via two big wood stoves and if I want to rouse them quickly on a cold morning I simply stuff them with sticks, get a little flicker going, close the stone doors and then aim a jet of WD through the air vent. The result is a bit like firing up a Saturn rocket – the stove sounds like one, and, if I kept my finger on the aerosol nozzle for long enough, it would eventually lift off like one.

There are lot of ancient floorboards in my house. I like the creak of them when I walk over them and I like the glow of the wood and the varying textures of the grain, but I would hate to have to continually polish them, as I know some folk do. Much better to give any scuffed

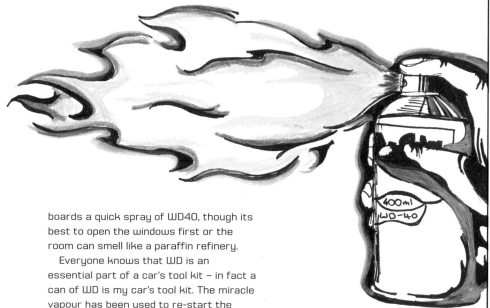

boards a quick spray of WD40, though its best to open the windows first or the room can smell like a paraffin refinery.

Everyone knows that WD is an essential part of a car's tool kit – in fact a can of WD is my car's tool kit. The miracle vapour has been used to re-start the engine after a flood drowned the electric's; it freed up jammed door locks, brake cylinders, clutch levers and handbrake cables; it somehow resurrected the seemingly defunct radio cassette player. Driving through a blizzard at night, one of the disc brakes locked up immovably with ice and packed slush. I was ten miles from home, but luckily I managed to coat the offending disc with a layer of "WD" and though I had to respray the disc after six miles as it had, by then, burnt off the lubricant, I made it back in one piece.

Of course, being a fisherman, I keep all my fishing reels spinning sweetly through a regular dose of "WD", but, of all its myriad uses, I think it's greatest Idler value must be as a shoe preserver. Almost ten years ago I bought – for £45 in a half-price sale – a very comfortable, light, well made pair of leather walking shoes. Since then, I have worn them almost every day in every season: I have worn them for fishing, tree-climbing, rock climbing, tennis (hard court), hiking and serious pub crawling (i.e. several miles between each pub). I have never cleaned them once, and yet, apart from slight fraying on the heel support they look today almost as good as new simply because I give them a weekly ten second burst of WD40. It's true that, before spraying, they can look a little tired and dusty, but the miracle "silicone free" droplets revive them instantly – and keep them 100% waterproof.

My kids treat their school shoes in the same manner and it's remarkable how worn, scruffy and cracked leather can be made to look so glossy and respectable with just a couple of idle squirts from the magic canister. 🔊

KIRK MOMENTS BEFORE DEFEATING A FRENCHMAN

IDLE PURSUITS:

FENCING: THE ART OF WAR

An interview with pro fencer Kirk Zavieh. By Dan Kieran

DAN: Where does fencing come from?

ZAVIER: I suppose as long as there have been swords there's been the practice. There is an Egyptian carving dating from 1200 BC showing a fight with masks, judges and modified swords.

The modern concept of fencing really started to take off in the 15th century – two fencing manuals were published in Spain and by the 16th century the rapier had grown in popularity across Europe as a duelling weapon. This heralded the era of fencing schools

– if you were unskilled and thought to express your opinion in public, the price was often death. By 1800s the fencing mask had arrived, ascribed to La Boessiere as a reaction to unintended rhinoplasty, along with a host of intricate rules and regulations that varied from Hungary, Spain, Austria, Germany, Italy and France. So the sport was born. It was one of the original sports at the Athens Olympics in 1904.

DAN: It has a reputation for being a bit of a posh sport, is it expensive to do?

KIRK: Here it was traditionally taught at public schools and hence has had that UK class thing about it but it's now so widely practiced I certainly wouldn't use the word posh.

In Europe both the old eastern European and western territories have viewed fencing as a good

KIRK, (SUITED, RIGHT) AND THE ALGERIAN OLYMPIC
TEAM AT BARCELONA IN 1992

opportunity to win Olympic medals. It has thus been supported there at a grass root level. There are several clubs in the UK and they are not expensive – less than any gym membership. The kit will cost you the best part of £150 (first-hand).

DAN: I'm learning to fence at the moment. After each lesson I can barely walk down a flight of stairs. Does the physical side of it get easier?

KIRK: Depends how old you are... And yes of course it does get easier – actually, not being able to go down stairs is a good sign, your muscles are rebuilding – it means you have been putting in the footwork.

DAN: My teacher tells me that in the old days you didn't actually hold a foil until you'd finished your first year of training. Now no-one can be bothered to wait that long, has this effected the "spirit" of fencing?

KIRK: The "Old days" he is referring to will probably be Hungarian or Russian. In Budapest, up to fifteen years ago, all you did if you wanted to be a fencer was footwork. You started at ten years old and would be desperate to be allowed to pick up a weapon. One day you might be selected for your national team and get to travel, you might even win a medal but only if you listened to your coach and watched carefully. Fencing in that sense wasn't just a sport or a hobby, it was everything, a way of life. It does not resonate in those countries in the same way today, perhaps in parts of the US where local clubs have bought the best Russian coaches who no doubt imbue their kids with that approach. That could be why last year's junior world champion was American.

DAN: The repetition of the physical movements is quite meditative, is that part of the attraction?

KIRK: Repetition is part of the process of learning technique (like say the piano) whereby you are able to move with control and changes of tempo as if it was natural. In my experience it is about concentrating, meditating sounds a bit areyuveda, if you think you are meditating while being trained by a great coach, prepare for a good slap.

DAN: How many different methods are there to learn?

KIRK: Firstly there are three weapons – Sabre – where you hit anything above the waist – you can cut with the blade; Epee – evolved from the rapier, an all-body target; and Foil - a thinner version of the epee – target above the waist.

In each weapon there are several styles – often characterized by nation. In Sabre, the Russians and Poles for example are very physical in their attack – open minded and not pre-meditated – almost response driven – counter-attacking while they attack – as if they were playing free jazz. The Hungarians on the other hand will plan an attack carefully – they are more classical, intricate and perfect. When a great Russian and Hungarian meet on a good day for both, say an Olympic final, then you will see magic.

DAN: Have you ever been tempted to grow a moustache?

KIRK: No. 🐌

Fencing kit suppliers:
www.duellist.com
Fencing lessons:
http://www.swashandbuckle.org.uk

IDLE PURSUITS:
IT'S COOL TO BE HOT

Will Hogan **builds his own sauna**

Some years ago, a good friend of mine was infatuated with Sauna's. Having been sent to document some Finnish music festival, he was taken by his grinning hosts to experience the full Finnish Sauna Culture.

The wholesome family activity complete with Ice-cold plunge dip, a few shots of lip pursing vodka and herrings gave him a magical insight into the salubrious properties of steaming out impurities and centering the mind in the all encompassing embrace of steam. The infatuation dried up rather abruptly when he tried to recreate these sensations in Bethnal Green Sauna in Hackney. He came back after one particular visit with a vexed look on his sweat-laden brow. The romantic image that he harboured had been somewhat sullied, as he gently awoke from a steam-induced slumber to the sight of some hirsute Hackney based gangster standing directly in front of him wielding a large erection. In spite of this, the Sauna – pronounced in Finnish Sow-na rather than the English Saw-na, is in my experience simply a magical event and one best completed with friends as opposed to strangers in the public forum. There is no better way to steam out the unpleasant accumulation of the week's stresses and the world's impurities than in this haven of tranquillity and warmth. Akin to a large wooden womb, you can't help but feel entirely foetus-like in it's cleansing vapours. It was with this in mind that I couldn't wait to visit my friend's home made construction and use this as inspiration to build my own 5 Vitna(star) Sauna.

Obviously the love of Sauna's and the not too distinct climate similarities to Britain were motivation enough for my friend Tom to build his Sauna in the spare outhouse in his garden. The sight of hapless suburbanites rolling around in the spring rain flagellating themselves with bits of birch may raise a few eyebrows in most back gardens, but not around his neck of the woods. I shared a sauna with him and here's a few tips that he imparted, many the result of bitter experience.

Let's begin with a few considerations: Firstly you need a good size space, this can be a garage, loft, cellar, box room or outhouse that should be at least 2-3 meters wide and 1.5-2 meters long (from front to back) though they can be smaller. The space must be at least 2150mm in height (which is actually smaller than the average domestic ceiling) There are five main areas to consider when constructing your own sauna:

1. The inner panelling or lining

The most important aspect of your Sauna is the wood you construct it with. Any type of wood other than the finest Abachi will warp hideously in the steamy environs of the Sauna, so this must be good imported timber (preferably) from Finland. The interior needs to accommodate benches: the wider the better – for reclining in comfort, so these should be at least 700mm wide and 2000mm long, fixed to the walls and not held up by supports on the ground. These must also be made

GET YOUR ROCKS ON

of Abachi to ensure optimum comfort and prevent body piercing splinters. Likewise nails and screws must not be used in the benches, to prevent thigh-scalding metal coming into contact with your precious skin.

2. The Vapour Barrier

This is required inside the inner panelling so that moisture cannot penetrate beyond the insulation. Again, using Finnish materials will yield best results and also prevent your Sauna developing the aroma of a sauna-builders bum crack.

3. The Framing and thermal insulation.

The framing is the backbone of the Sauna. If your sauna is to be built into an existing structure you'll only need to do this horizontally to provide the gap for the Rockwool to insulate the inner panelling. The sauna needs to be framed above the ground and away from the surrounding walls to ensure decent insulation and to prevent your heating bill resembling the national debt of Columbia.

4. The outer finish

The outer finish should be constructed of the same wood as the interior (if freestanding) or you won't have to worry about this if your sauna is in an existing room or structure. To the sauna obsessive authenticity is of paramount importance, but by all means slap on a bit of pebbledash if you want to merge seamlessly with your surroundings.

5. Internal apparatus – Heater (Kauti) lights, stereo etc

You'll need a decent heater but ventilation is all important too. This ensures a circulation of fresh, steamable air. You'll also come out of the sauna alive. Lights are also a requisite, under bench dim lighting is *de rigeur* but make sure you use well-insulated wire to prevent an unwanted "fry-up".

A full, luxury DIY sauna can be put together for around £1000 or you can pay around £2000 for a "pre built" model.

For all things Sauna related contact: ABLagerholm.co.uk. They're the don's. Thanks to Axel Thill for picture of his sauna. You can log onto his site via the ABLagerholm webpage.

TEA TIME:
WHEN TEA IS A MATTER OF LIFE AND DURGTH

Chris Yates discovers Happy Tea
Illustration by Claire Hatcher

Durgth" is the word you breath noxiously out when a concerned friend, wondering why you sound so feeble on the phone, asks you how you are feeling. You haven't got the energy to enunciate properly and so the reply is: "A-feel...like durgth..."

You shouldn't have gone to the pub the previous night because you knew something biologically hostile was brewing in you – something you might easily have overcome had you forced yourself to have an early night and a double aspirin. But now, with the body having to battle on three fronts – excess alcohol, exhaustion (you didn't get home till 4am) and flu, you just want to die quietly and without fuss. "Shall I come round and make you a nice cup of tea?" Asks the sympathetic friend. Tea? You think. Ugh! You couldn't face it. At least, you wouldn't want even the weakest most inoffensive cup of ordinary tea. Yet there is a tea that you could take, one that would not only refresh you, but also save you from oblivion.

I discovered the recipe for this anti-death potion in an old book of herbs and herbal remedies. The author had travelled the world seeking out obscure plants and discovering all kinds of wondrous applications for them. It was only at the end of the book that, almost like an afterthought, the author set down a recipe for an herbal infusion that had been offered to him during an arduous journey across India. It was, he wrote, the ideal tonic for a weary traveller as it possessed a perfect combination of ingredients to revive the body, refresh the mind and soothe the spirit. At the time of first reading this book, I too had just returned from an arduous journey – through a grim night of food poisoning, so naturally I was willing to try anything that might restore my interior – even herbal tea.

A good woman was sent on a mission to Culpeppers, the herbalists and the ingredients were brought to me steaming in a teapot. I sipped the strange brew and – almost instantly – it worked and I was alive again. Furthermore, I really liked the taste: fragrant, but earthy; soft round the edges but with a firm clean centre. Within the hour I was climbing to the top of a high hill to throw a frisbee into the breeze.

This remarkable potion contains four herbs: camomile, lime blossom, peppermint and vervain – a pinch of equal parts brewed in a pot for four to five minutes. You can buy all these ingredients in tea bag form, except the vervain, but I prefer to have any kind of tea as loose leaf and so a trip to Culpeppers is the only option for me.

According to the herbalist, the benefits of the four constituents are thus: Camomile, good for the nervous system; Lime also; vervain, a cure for insomnia; Peppermint cleanses the digestive system as well as being mildly antiseptic, "destroying germs and preventing putrescent changes." Vervain is the iron in the soul of this tea, restoring the body's equilibrium through its "miraculous influence on the vital organs." Trouble is, last time I went to Culpeppers and the local health food store they didn't have any more vervain. Has someone else cornered the market? Has it been banned by the EU because it poses a threat to the profits of the pharmaceutical industries?

The name of this tea is, appropriately, Happy Tea. As well as a life saver, it makes a perfect night-cap, guaranteeing not only a restful sleep but also wondrous dreams. I've come to prefer it to coffee as an after dinner beverage and I might even try it one day as an alternative to ordinary black tea with my breakfast. But I must always remember to keep a reserve supply in case of emergencies, when I or my four wild children might need it for occasional physical or spiritual nose dives.

Happy Tea: It will raise you from the dead, and at all other times, when you're not dead, it will raise your spirits-and your game. ☻

THE PASSENGER:
DRIVING ME SANE

Fanny Johnstone climbs into the driving seat at last

I've just discovered the most brilliant way of getting a car for free. All you have to do is to be more useless than anyone else in your family. It's great. You'll love it.

Here's what I did. As a bird I've done my fair share of miles in Ferraris, Porsches, Challenger II tanks, tractors, Ford Cortinas, Dodge Magnums, hot rods, stretch Limousines, Volvos, Citroen DSs, DB5s, E-types, New York cabs, Mercedes 280s etcetera. And not always in the back seat either. (It's pretty easy by the way. You just say "Wow I love your car. Can I have a ride?" And yes occasionally you may have to flash your USP to get a foot in the door, but generally men love it. It doesn't always work well with women drivers by the way, except on the chicks in Miami, so if you're a single guy or a gay bird go to Florida and have a go).

Anyway I'd always expected that one day, when I'd written enough brilliant articles to afford it, I'd own something suitably me. Something very Fanny. Something that I could drive with a disingenuousness air that would reek of me thinking, "Gosh is this really me pulling up outside The Coach & Horses in this Dodge Magnum Charger? I'm terribly sorry be so flamboyantly cool. The handsome brute of a car sort of crept up on me and, well, we fell in love and there we are. Excuse me a moment while I reverse it out of that wall I've just crashed into, and please don't tell the landlord until I've had a chance to charm him". And then, with a certain vile guile, I'd

have to climb out of the window in my vintage Levis and white Daisy Duke boots, and run.

So it should have come as no surprise then, being the sort of bird who was too busy riding around in fast cars to write the brilliant articles in the first place, and who couldn't come up with any better fantasy than the jaded Daisy Duke one, that I ended up getting my first car by inheriting it from my grandmother. When my grandfather died recently she decided that it was time to buy herself a new car and so, as I was noticeably the only person in the family who was still too poor to buy a car, she decided to give her old one to me. "Look after it, Fan," she said, patting its bonnet. "It's been very good to me." I promised I would and that was that. The car and I set off and got to know each other.

It didn't take long. It's white. It's a Vauxhall Corsa. It's an L Reg. It's got a 1,196 cc engine. Its clutch squeaks. And, er, that was about it.

Or at least, I thought it was. But the next time I got into it – wearing my vintage jeans and white Daisy Duke boots, tearfully aware that some part of me had failed because all I owned now was an inherited Vauxhall Corsa – I was hit by the over-riding smell of my grandparents, dog. Phoof. It was like a rescue remedy for no-hopers. That marinated doggy smell made me remember going for walks around Great Windsor Park with my grandparents, listening to the comforting stories my grandfather would tell about

THE VAUXHALL CORSA

idiots he'd known that had come good, and the do-gooders that had become idiots. And I thought fondly of my grandmother driving a million times to the shops in it with her wicker basket on the back seat. And that when Grandpa was ill my grandmother must have driven him to and from the hospital in the car, and after the funeral generally busied herself around England in it. And so instead of playing at Daisy Duke, I started yearning for one of those very British tartan travel rugs just like my grandparents used to have. And in place of a crate of Bud in the trunk and engine power that makes you horny, I was happy with a thermos of sugared tea and the fact that it didn't shake much when we travelled at 90mph.

Did this mean I'd given up on life? Did this mean that I'd never aim to have a Dodge Magnum because the Vauxhall would breed complacency? Did my actually buying the tartan travel rug (soft orange and green from a 100% wool shop in Cumbria, yummy) mean that I was eerily becoming my grandmother? No. It just meant I could get to assignments I might never have made it to before, and that I was discovering a new-found love of all things English that I'd forgotten along the way.

I love the way the Corsa struggles up hills but yippees down the other side. You can tell that it thinks driving south to Cornwall is all downhill. I love the fact that no-one will bother burgling a Vauxhall Corsa whose sticker reads 'I brake for pasties' on the rear window. I love the uncompromisingly dull dashboard design with no extra features. I love the glove compartment stuffed with biscuits from the Greek shop on Moscow Road and the Simpsons wet-wipes from that spooky chemist in Windermere. I love the fact that it's so tweedy and naff that I don't have to struggle against the cool. People can laugh and I don't care. I love the squeaky clutch and its fanning system which works, while all around me faster cars overheat and break down on the A303. I love the fact that it was free and that Grandpa would have approved of my pleasure as he was the most frugal gentleman I ever knew.

Most of all I love that when I'm feeling scared, because I'm grown-up and don't like it, I can go and sit in the car, listen to the Top 40 and pretend I'm 10 again. If I close my eyes I can just about smell my grandfather's cherry pipe tobacco as he approaches the car. ☻

IDLE PURSUITS:
CLOUDS OF GLORY

Tim Richardson on the noble cigar
Illustration by Linda Scott

As I was saying to my wife only the other day while pulling on one of my favourite Romeo y Julieta Cedros Deluxe No.2s, I think it was R. L. Stevenson who observed, "No woman should marry a man who does not smoke." She had some difficulty hearing my *bon mot*, however, since she was in the kitchen and I was in the garden, and the door was only slightly ajar due to the freezing weather conditions. It is difficult to justify the all-pervading fug emitted by even the smallest cheroot in a modern household which is otherwise non-smoking, especially if there are small children on the premises. Hence the *al fresco* situation.

However, domestic complications should not stop us from enjoying one of the noblest and most transcendent pleasures available to man or woman, because for those who have the stomach for it, a good cigar is a passport to a reverie that is edifying rather than inebriated, a world of the imagination where fleeting thoughts tumble over each other and then meld into one, before tearing themselves apart and drifting off into nothingness like smoke itself.

A cigar can perhaps best be enjoyed solo – which is how I have taken about 90% of mine in fifteen years' of smoking them – but among like-minded friends a batch of cigars will change the atmosphere and rhythm of the situation, as each person tends to their own firestick, unconsciously editing their own pronouncements and recieving everyone else's with an easy agreeableness that is unusual in other situations. It is as if the smoke from the cigars – so much thicker and more potent than that from mere cigarettes – enfolds and enwraps the party in an insubstantial and odiferous duvet of bonhomie, cushioning them from quotidian depredations and the common imbecility of their companions. As Thomas Carlyle put it, "Tobacco-smoke is the one element in which, by our European manners, men can sit silent together without embarrassment, and where no man is bound to speak one word more than he has actually and veritably got to say."

It probably sounds a little like smoking cannabis (except for the imbecility part), but to my mind a cigar is a much deeper and more complex experience than that. At the risk of sounding corny, the kind of transcendency it inspires is probably more akin to Ecstasy

As the smoke swirls about your person, it not only renders you invisible to others, but also obscures you from yourself

than anything else in the world of proscribed drugs, although with a cigar of course one is not lumbered with any of the crazy stuff. A cigar may make you dance all night, but it will be a stately and complicated fandango, not some double-quick two-step. The only side-effect of cigar-smoking that I have noticed is most welcome: extraordinarily vivid and pleasant dreams. I once smoked a cigar after a day botanizing in the hills of Madeira, and dreamed all night of brilliant flowers blooming and bursting in slow-motion all round me like underwater fireworks.

Where to start; what to buy? Most cigar smokers agree that it has to be a Havana: nothing else measures up, whatever patriotic Americans afflicted by the trade embargo on Cuba might say. All proper cigars are expensive (from about £7.50 to £12 each), so you might as well go for the most expensive, right? (More

financial advice later.) Consumption is minimal: the habit of chainsmoking cigars is disgusting and vulgar, and most people enjoy one only after dinner or occasionally lunch. They are to be avoided on an empty stomach, as they can be overpowering; a cigar hangover is a real and present danger.

The cigar shop is the best place to buy, and London has always been the destination for the best-quality cigars outside Havana. It is perfectly all right to buy just one cigar, and the assistants in shops like Fox's of St James's are friendly enough despite their grand addresses. The airport shops have good-quality stock and offer savings, but you have to buy by the boxful (25 cigars). You can save a lot of money buying abroad: the most reliable foreign source is Spain, although I have noticed that there can still be a difference between the quality of cigars made for the Spanish market and the British market. You can pick up cigars in silver tubes from off-licences in upmarket areas, but it is well to harbour low expectations of these, since the cigar will probably be too dry unless the place sells a lot of cigars and the stock is regularly replenished.

In the cigar shop, the done thing is to select your own cigar, or else trust the assistant to do it for you (I only let them do this if they are at least fifty years old). Cigars come in a confusing array of colours, lengths and widths, and none of these factors is a guide to strength of cigar. It is best to ask for advice if you have not checked in *The Cigar Companion* (Apple Books) first. The cigar should be unblemished, its outer leafwrapper completely intact; it should give a little when you squeeze it and certainly not crackle. Of the major brands, a Bolivar will be strong and uncompromising; a Cohiba

(Castro's fabled brand) is complex and robust; a torpedo-shaped Cuaba (launched in 1996) is medium strength, slow to get going but excellent value; an H. Upmann is also good value, mild but of variable quality; a Punch is spicy and quite light; a Hoyo de Monterrey is rich yet delicate (the double corona is a king among cigars); a Montecristo is uniquely flavoured, oily and aromatic; a Partagas is earthy and straightforward; and a Romeo y Julieta is medium-strength and reliable at all sizes. I buy a box or two a year, and singles to ring the changes or experiment with new brands.

Now to the smoking. You need a cigar cutter to cut the end off – Cubans apparently bite theirs, but this is probably possible because the cigar is much more supple in its native land. Biting a cigar in Britain will probably ruin it. When I am caught without a cigar cutter, I saw the end off slowly with a serrated knife. It is best to light your own cigar, and let others do so, too. Hold the cigar in the hand, not the mouth, and let the flame play around the whole diameter of the cigar for ten seconds or so, before taking a drag to get it going. The golden rule is: never inhale. This is what catches out cigarette smokers, and generally renders them incapable of enjoying cigars. You can take big puffs or small puffs, a little or often, and finish the cigar as soon as you have had enough, even if it is half-smoked. A cigar takes a while to get going, and one's relationship with it deepens with time. As the narcotic effect of the tobacco takes effect, it also gets gradually stronger, leading to a state of nirvana by about halfway to two-thirds of the way down the cigar.

What should one do while smoking a cigar? Just sitting there is probably the best option, although poetry and music can be appreciated in new ways under the influence. Recently I have favoured Horace's *Odes*, which seem to capture the cigar-smoker's mood of imaginative but never embittered reflection of his own lot. A holiday often presents wonderful opportunities for cigar-smoking, perhaps accompanied by some local liquor for added piquancy. For a more exciting cigar-smoking environment, a bullfight cannot be bettered. A cigar smoked during a *corrida* at one of the great bullrings, such as the Maestranza in Seville, seems to complement the rhythm of this beautiful meditation on death. At any event, a cigar lit in an environment with no opportunity for philosophical thoughts is, to my mind, a cigar wasted, a habituation of the nicotine addict rather than the true aficionado.

The thoughts of that aficionado, mid-cigar, are many and strange, and impossible for an observer – breathing normal air like an untroubled sheep or pig – to fathom. As the smoke swirls about your person, it not only renders you invisible to others but also obscures you from yourself. A cigar allows you to transcend your own being, to look down on yourself and your situation with the amused detachment of a benevolent god. You find yourself following one train of thought, only to have it spark off in another direction entirely with a peculiar clarity, never the random swirling of alcoholic inebriation. A cigar engenders an intensely satisfying feeling of irresponsible intellectual escapism: all of one's "best" ideas and sternest resolutions occur during the inward conversations conjured by cigar smoke. But the best thing is, when the reverie has passed, you will have no recollection of what any of those ideas or resolutions were. ◉

John Cheever
RICHARD FORD
RICHARD FORD
THE ULTIMATE GOOD LUCK
A MAGGOT
JOHN FOWLES
JOHN FOWLES
DANIEL MARTIN
JONATHAN FRANZEN
COLD MOUNTAIN
ELLMANN
JAMES JOYCE
James Joyce
Randall Jarrell
Angels
DENIS JOHNSON
Kafka's clothes
Kafka
CORMAC McCARTHY
CORMAC McCARTHY
SEEING MANY PLAIN
IAN McEWAN
THE INNOCENT
IAN McEWAN
McGRATH
DANUBE
The TIME of our TIME
NORMAN MAILER
AMOS OZ
TIM PARKS
TIM PEARS
IN A LAND OF PLENTY
PEREC
Life A User's Manual
PERKINS
JOHN UPDIKE
JOHN UPDIKE
Luongo

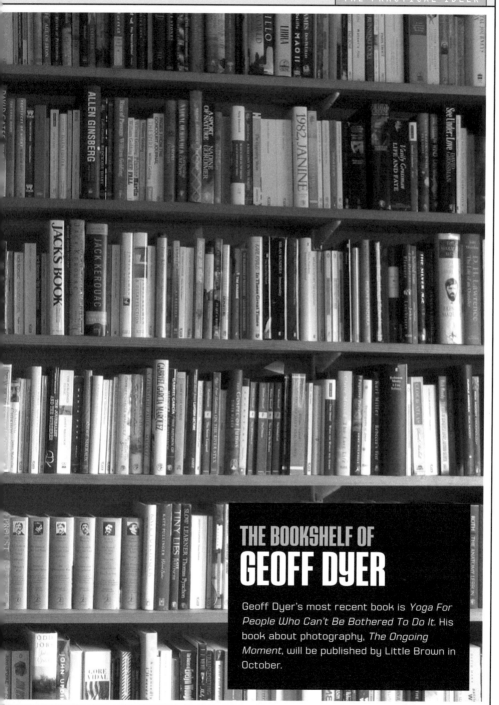

THE BOOKSHELF OF
GEOFF DYER

Geoff Dyer's most recent book is *Yoga For People Who Can't Be Bothered To Do It*. His book about photography, *The Ongoing Moment*, will be published by Little Brown in October.

THE BROWSER:
JEFF LINT'S SNAIL CAMP

Steve Aylett reviews the work of cult author Jeff Lint

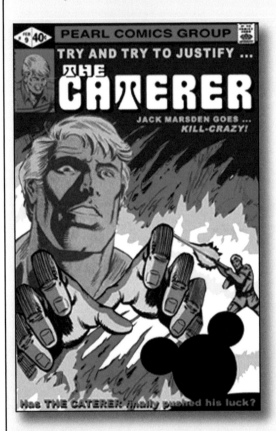

THE CATERER, LINT'S PEARL COMICS CLASSIC

Most of us have wondered at one time or another what the appeal of Jeff Lint's work is. The same strengths of his works are cited again and again by enthusiastic readers – a tribute to the consistency of his talent. That Lint is a builder of monsters so pointless and detailed that one could almost strangle him for wasting our time,

this is obvious. That he is a master of exposing quite different human weaknesses than are normally dealt with in fiction or anywhere else, so different that he must often invent a new term for the failing (e.g. "cren"), is a matter of record. That he is a tentacle-obsessive who is simultaneously exhausted and scampering, tubby and lean, welcome and inconvenient; that he creates characters that display an unrealistically high level of combustibility, to the point that they will explode into flame when a match is merely shown to them, to those of us who read his novels and short stories this is no revelation.

What draws us into the worlds that Lint creates are his wayward protagonists. Certainly they are baleful and, far from being unassailable supermen, are often asleep, not easily awoken with a single shake, and sometimes given to throttling those who attempt it. In some books (e.g. *Fanatique*) the protagonist will disappear for several pages while the book goes on, and then re-enter it without any explanation of where he's been (probably asleep or saying halloo to a dog). These heroes and heroines are a parallel breed: their motivations are obvious to themselves and alien to the average reader. Through Lint's pen we watch already strange characters become increasingly vivid individuals who are so much their own creature that when the crux of a certain social/scientific/cosmic matter occurs, they are elsewhere doing something far more interesting and barely aware of the fashionable crisis. They would be the last to put effort into deciding the fates of others, as the worlds and societies around them seem quite insincere about desiring to change. On the rare occasion that a Lint hero does change something (as in "An Ominous Mirth") everyone protests, agitated and embarrassed, because when they said they wanted the change made they assumed it was impossible. For the Lint hero, unlike the heroes of ancient myth, the unavoidable confrontation with his own nature occurs at the beginning or before the story starts, and he is first discovered sitting on the burning shell of a car, wearing some sort of seaweed bonnet and playing a lute. Even the mimsy and ineffective Alan Jay is first seen riding a tiger shark up an embankment and doing a double forward-flip into a barbecue to which he was not invited.

We find a fine Lintian hero in Benny Mena. Benny, the protagonist in the tale "Snail Camp" (first published in pulp mag *Baffling Stories*), spends his young years in an oppressive environment. He must eat nine hundred snails every day, including the shells, and have his performance rated according to criteria

STEVE AYLETT'S ISSUE OF ALAN MOORE'S BRILLIANT NEW COMIC, TOM STRONG (NO. 27) IS IN THE SHOPS NOW. OR YOU CAN WAIT FOR THE NEXT ANNUAL FROM AMERICA'S BEST COMICS.

that nobody understands. Unbeknownst to his friends and colleagues in Snail Camp, he has learnt the snails' language and must endure their screams and entreaties. Though comfortable, existence in Snail Camp is dreary and mindless. There is no discussion of travel, growth or discovery; in Benny's world such things are considered mere fripperies, the musings of a spooky and selfish child. Benny attempts to find out whether, if he stops eating snails or perhaps eats them in a "sarcastic" way, he will be merely banished or actually punished. To find out, he knocks out a colleague and accuses him of sleeping, then places a snail "spy" on the boy's back. The boy is taken away and, several months later, the snail returns saying

I SUPPOSE I SHOULD WARN YOU THIS ISN'T REALLY A PICNIC: I INTEND TO GO ON A SMALL KILLING SPREE. GODS WILL BE DRAGGED SCREAMING FROM THE ETHER. HOLD THIS FOR ME WILL YOU? YES, HISTORY REPEATS ITSELF AND IF YOU OBSERVE, YOU CAN TELL THAT IT'S GETTING REALLY BORED NOW.

LINT TELLS IT LIKE IT IS: THE CATERER (FROM THE COLLECTION OF STEVE AYLETT)

that the boy was perversely rewarded by banishment. The hero falls asleep, is banished, and later returns with a neutron bomb.

It might be said that "Snail Camp" is a standard-issue everyman tale, showing the too-close-to-see manipulations in our work-a-day existence, where nothing new is permitted and yet truth is simultaneously deplored as a pre-colonised territory. But Benny presents us with a more optimistic picture of ourselves: a chubby moron who stumbles through existence until the facts bite off part of his nose. Herein lies the essence of a true hero, the kind that Lint so easily creates, be it Felix Arkwitch or Valac of the novel Jelly Result. As Lint scholar Eileen Welsome has said, "seeing the underpinnings of the world at all times, he finds himself to be terribly frank and unpopular wherever he goes."

Lewis Tambs has described Lint's fiction as "Bitter Baroque": "His protagonists traffic in casually relentless honesty in the face of four thousand years of layered lies and evasion strategy. They like an opportunity to do something confoundedly strange, but they prefer to have the rare-as-white-gold peace to get on with their own projects, and occasionally some jam." Serge Brunner of Lint's novel *I Am A Centrifuge* must make such constant allowances while moving through society's vacuum of evasion that he is effectively using his own skull as a sort of space helmet. That character too demonstrates the combination of obtusely-timed lethargy and pyrotechnical effrontery that make the Lintian hero so inaccessible and appealing to his readers.

In the words of Benny Mena as he watches the obliteration of Snail Camp, "If all governments were combined, we could save on travel and gunpowder." Accusation or guidebook to cultural delight? You decide. ☻

Steve Aylett's book about the life and books of Jeff Lint, LINT, is published by Thunder's Mouth Press in May 2005.

THE BROWSER:
ANARCHY IN ALDGATE E1

The *Idler* visited the Freedom Bookshop in London's East End
to see what they're reading

Tucked down an alley next door to the Whitechapel Art Gallery in the East End of London, the Freedom Bookshop is one of the UK's hidden treasures. The largest anarchist bookshop in the country, this is where to come if you want a copy of anything from a pamphlet edition of the *Unabomber Manifesto* to *A Short History of Anarchism* (the condensed, English-translation version of Max Nettlau's nine volume, German-language *History of Anarchism*). Currently popular titles include *We Are Everywhere: The Irresistible Rise of Global Anti-capitalism* (Verso, £10.99), and *Our Word is Our Weapon*, the collected writings of Subcomandante Insurgente Marcos, edited by Juan Ponce de Lyon (Serpent's Tail, £14.99). Freedom Press is also a publisher in its own right, and among the recent titles they've brought out is Tony Allen's *A Summer In The Park: A Journal Of Speakers' Corner* in which Allen, a soap box veteran himself, talks about the bizarre experience of being a semi-official heckler, teaching tourists and the reticent how to engage in arguments and banter with the speakers who congregate in the north east corner of Hyde Park, London. 🐚

FREEDOM BOOKSHOP
Angel Alley, 84b Whitechapel High Street, London E1 7QX www.freedompress.org.uk

Further reading from Freedom Press:
Why Work: Arguments for the Leisure Society (which includes Bertrand Russell's "In Praise of Idleness"), Freedom Press, £6.95 and *About Anarchism*, Nicholas Walter, Freedom Press, £4.20

EASY SOUNDS:

ON THE SICK

He's mad and he don't care. Joe Piercy meets DJ Unfit For Work

I first met Phil Murphy (aka DJ Unfit For Work) in the mid 1980s. Around this time I was in the process of receiving my marching orders from Art School and half-heartedly trying to start a band. Phil, for his part, had a band and a very good band they were too. The Regular Guys wrote heartbreaking pop songs, witty and wise, scything guitars and scathing lyrics that raged against the smug complacency of Thatcherism and the yuppie utopian dream. After a handful of highly memorable singles and with major labels sniffing around waving their chequebooks, The Regular Guys split up. The reasons for their demise have never been entirely clear, although Murphy's long battle with mental illness and subsequent nervous breakdown can certainly be read in mitigation.

And so they slipped into obscurity, other bands trod a similar path and received more acclaim but few have had the same acid sharp intensity. Murphy's mental condition deteriorated and sadly, support of friends and loved ones aside (in particular, lawyer girlfriend Claire Williams), most of the next decade was punctuated by various stints in institutions. People would talk occasionally, in hushed reverent tones about the genius that lost its way. Various myths sprang up about him and the nature of his madness, new projects or collaborations that he may or may not be working on but from Murphy himself there was only silence. He became a sort of Syd Barrett of the Brighton underground music scene; name checked by such luminaries as Julian Cope and Steve Albini; an absent maverick who was unable to escape his own private hell.

Until now that is. Spurred on by his contacts with The Mad Pride organisation (people he claims he had no choice but to associate with during his time in what he blithely describes as "various nut houses") Murphy started writing and recording again last year. The result of this endeavour is an album released under the name of DJ Unfit For Work titled "Still Alive L.A.M.F." on The Mad Pride label. A sprawling dream pop epic that mixes coruscating guitars, analogue electronica and shimmering pianos to provide a perfect soundtrack to Murphy's fragile, plaintive laments. I met up with Murphy recently for the first time in many years to discuss the DJ Unfit For Work album, his association with Mad Pride and, well, anything that came into his head and few things that didn't. He is always witty and erudite and gives a good

account of someone you wouldn't associate with having spent so long gazing into the abyss, although his frequent slips into street-smart argot can be somewhat disquieting.

IDLER: In the *Daily Mail* sense, a lot of the "Mad Pride" group are economically "idle". What do you do to while away the hours?

UNFIT FOR WORK: Different stuff, ya know? Kinda of mood-dependent. In Mad Pride we've got a fairly extreme mixture of artists, aesthetes, revolutionaries and ne'er do well lumpen types. None of us seem to salivate at the prospect of "Windows 2000 Spreadsheets" or souped-up "basket-weaving" classes in dreary day centres! Many do, however, salivate at the prospect of sex, recreational drugs and art. We all got a bit sex-crazed last year and some – myself included – got into "swinging". It tailed off a bit when the cold weather snapped in, although I hasten to add we drew the line at "dogging" in the Stan Collymore sense! The first time we got the nerve up for a "collective" approach was in this large Victorian house in Camden. I won't deny there was a giggly embarrassment factor all round at first, but after a few lines and several vodkas all round most of us got into it. It was a totally amazing way to spend an afternoon – well better than "Countdown" at any rate! Mainly though the twosomes, or in one case threesomes, involved went into separate rooms. The big "group" concept as such never came about. So much for collective consciousness and the joining of body and mind.

IDLER: There seems to be common strands running through your songs, from The Regular Guys through to DJ Unfit For Work, in particular a strong disgust for the clichés of social register – such as the transparency of certain types of conversation, be it pub chat up routines or politically correct posturing. However, there seems to be genuine sadness that social interaction is often reduced to a bland and repetitive stream of signifiers. Is insincerity akin to a social disease or malevolent virus that alienates us from our peers?

UNFIT FOR WORK: My main aim with The Regular Guys and now with DJ Unfit For Work is to produce music of such power that it brooks no opposition. In real life I'm often playing catch-up with "the normals" so its vital to my self-worth that I totally out-perform them and demoralise them, in terms of musical competition, in the domain where I am stronger than them. Fortunately I have the ability to do this. Social "inauthenticity" doesn't bother me much. Small talk, rituals, dress codes etc, they can be fun if they oil the wheels of communication. In fact the worst song in living memory is the God-awful "Once In A Lifetime" by the God-awful David Byrne. That attempts to pick up on an outdated form of – er – "alienation". Pseudo outsiders are a pain in the arse – none more so than Byrne and his ilk. "Whose is this beautiful car"!? "Whose is this beautiful house"!? They're YOURS you cunt! What's the fucking problem!

IDLER: Another common theme is love, or rather the lack of it in everyday life. Do you set out to write about love as an unattainable goal? Or are you more interested in the absence/loss of love as a fundamental human value but a value that can still be reclaimed?

UNFIT FOR WORK: Love is certainly not unattainable for many. I certainly am not hostile to it and were, say, Helena Bonham Carter to read this and find those feelings welling up she would be welcome to pursue me with undue vigour and little risk of rebuff. Freud and the post-Freudians were incorrect to label love as "necessary". People cannot survive without food and shelter. Unfortunately many people have to survive without love. The current Western obsession of course is "desire". Love is often disparaged by our cultural milieu as the "sad" recourse of those without the "looks-power" to have their true desire met. I feel love can be a fantastic thing in all kinds of contexts including, but not limited to, gay or straight couples, families of various kinds and friends. Whether it automatically "must" at all times take precedence over all other social constructs I think is doubtful. But it is a more humane concept than "family" to orientate towards.

IDLER: You haven't worked for many years and your intermittent bouts of illness resulted in lengthy periods of disability benefit or "on the sick", so to speak. Given that the Blair government has pledged to crackdown on disability benefit, how has being removed from the grim treadmill of the workplace informed your music? Furthermore, what is the response of Mad Pride to these worrying Government initiatives?

UNFIT FOR WORK: We intend to glamourise it but to be honest there are times when I'd rather have permanent genital herpes than be mad. But, like those nauseating motivational managers and, increasingly, Premiership football coaches, I try to look for "the positives". Clinical depression and anxiety with suicidal ideation is far from ideal as a lifestyle choice. As a songwriter and producer though, it is certainly a major plus.

IDLER: [slightly confused] Erm. And why might that be?

UNFIT FOR WORK: Why? The fact is unless a song or sound is brilliant, at least in some way, it has no positive impact on my mood. Because of this I only buy great records and I only write great songs. Anxiety with an obsessive component has worked for me too in terms of commodity fetishism. I've ended up either owning or – through other obsessives I know – and I'm talking about the full-on psychiatrically labelled here – having access to top line audio equipment, vintage and modern.

IDLER: Given the highly dubious provisions of the Mental Health Act, Do you feel we are regressing back to an almost pre-Victorian approach to Mental health issues, to a new age of what Foucault described as "The Great Confinement", whereby the state identifies potentially dissenting elements in society as deviant and therefore insane and removes them from public view – a kind of "mad woman in the attic" approach?

UNFIT FOR WORK: Foucault? That tosser! To be fair, though, I respect Lefties, despite their "me too" reasoning and anti-empirical theories. I get a buzz from reading the work of Ben Watson even though he once "offered me out". Nothing in this world is more important than weakening fascism by all means necessary and Lefties at least *intend* to be anti-fascist and I find their zeal and bravery highly erotic. I'm only human, after all.

IDLER: In the past you have been known to reserve particular disgust for the Left's band-wagon hijacking of any micro-

political issue that happens to be currently on the agenda. I'm interested to know when your position softened in this respect.

UNFIT FOR WORK: What are you? Some kind of cunt? Unlike the "me too" Left I don't have a problem with America intervening against fascism as it did in World War Two, Bosnia, Kosovo and Iraq. American foreign policy excesses cannot be tolerated but there is no equivalent to state sponsored fascist terror. The longer that twat Saddam is locked up in that bespoke disused khazi the better. Philosophically I've been checking the Critical Realists and Normblog. Mad Prides anarchist politics are on www.madpride.org. The socialist twist is on militantesthetix.com which is a beautiful site in every sense run by Ben Watson and Esther Leslie. The new Mental Health Bill is sewage, plain and simple. The state and the shrinks have all the power they need already to protect us all from sword meisters and axe wielders and to be fair the psychiatric profession has said as much. Mad Pride meets regularly with National M I N D fat cats and unfortunately the Bill is a done deal despite broad-spectrum opposition. But opposition will continue – BELIEVE!

The interview was terminated at this point as DJ Unfit For Work was becoming increasingly agitated. ◉

Still Alive – L.A.M.F. by DJ Unfit For Work is available from Mad Pride, C/O BM Active, London WC1N. DJ Unfit For Work will be playing a series of live shows in London in September 2005

EASY SOUNDS:
TAKING CARE OF BUSINESS

Former pop star John Moore describes how he seized the means of production and put out his own record

As a few of you might be aware, I have taken it upon myself to release another record. It's not as if the world was crying out for it, or that its non-existence would lead to a gaping chasm in popular culture. It was just something that was important to me. Something of a vanity project – although I fancy it'll be well regarded when I'm gone.

Having been thrown a financial lifeline by Rough Trade Records, as Black Box Recorder's adventure reached crisis point – not as a recording artist, but as press officer – I found myself in the fortunate position of having access to certain facilities unavailable to the common man, and a little insider information that could have changed things drastically had I known it before. Firstly, record manufacturing – if you know the right people – is as cheap as chips. Secondly, people in the music industry are not Mensa tie wearing, svengali sociopaths (not where I work at least). They are there because they – for whatever misguided reason, like music.

Anyway. Having spent more than half a year ensconced in rural Berkshire in a boathouse on the River Lodden, recording Sergeant Thriller's Darkside Petsounds Club, trying the patience of just about everybody who's ever known me, and going massively overdrawn at the goodwill bank, I'd just about given up hope of it seeing the light of day. All I wanted was for some borderline inadequate who'd traded human relationships in for business acumen to spot me a few Ks in return for a masterpiece. Nothing doing. In a way, it had served it's purpose as it was. I knew it was good, and at least I'd got it out of my system. Now I could get on with being an estate agent, news agent, secret agent etc... whatever it took to pay the mortgage.

However, on a slow afternoon last December, I sneaked a look at the books at Rough Trade. A total revelation. I realised that with a bit of manipulation and begging, I could get this Half Awake monstrosity manufactured for less than the price of a binge at the Colony Room. A thousand copies pressed by the factory who did The Strokes, The Libertines etc, at the same rate the company pay for pressing half a million. This works out at about forty-five pence each. One of the biggest parasites in the music industry is of course the press company. I'm a press officer. Now I am the artist, the label, the PR... I'll be ripping myself off if I'm not careful. True capitalism. I've joined the e-association, which is not a drug appreciation society, but the provider of barcodes. My records have their own barcode. I have my own label, The Germ Organization. I might even branch out into aviation soon.

Black Box Recorder were lazy sods. We liked money very much, especially if we didn't have to do much to get it, but if we'd put our own records out... if Sarah had worked the computer, Luke the phone and I'd driven the van, we'd be rich. ◉

TRAVEL:
HOLIDAY IN CAMBODIA

Actually, Julian Watson lives there and you won't find a
country less afflicted by the work ethic
Illustrations by Jeff Harrison

Rudyard Kipling had Burma on
his mind when he felt "sick 'o
wastin' leather on these
gritty pavin'-stones, An' the
blasted English drizzle wakes the
fever in my bones". But he did
recommend "...somewheres east
of Suez, where the best is like
the worst, Where there ain't no
Ten Commandments an' a man
can raise a thirst." For the
foreigner, or Barang as the
Cambodians call us, the lure of
Indochina is irresistible once
tasted. Other countries in the
area have their attractions.
Motives for visiting or even
staying can be mixed or better
still forgotten completely as by
Thomas Fowler in Graham
Greene's *The Quiet American*:
"They say you come to Vietnam,
you understand a lot in a few
minutes but the rest has got to
be lived. The smell. That is the
first thing that hits you,
promising everything in
exchange for your soul: And the
heat: your shirt is straight away
rag. You can hardly remember
your name or what you came to
escape from. But at night there
is a breeze. The river is beautiful.
You could be forgiven for
thinking... that only pleasure
matters. A pipe of opium or the

touch of a girl who might tell you she loves you."
There are those who would argue that Laos is the
apogee of idling countries in the region. Norman
Lewis described the French administrators as
"successful lobotomies – untroubled and mildly
libidinous," but I would advise all but the most
confident and experienced to try Cambodia first.
Be sure you like the red wines of Beaujolais before
drinking deep of the Rhône.

Cambodia slumbers between two hopelessly
busy countries – the rampant capitalist tiger of
Thailand and the savage pseudo-communist
crocodile of Vietnam. Almost unheard of until
America decided and failed to bomb it into
capitalism and that supreme enemy of idleness,
Pol Pot, tried to torture its people into Maoism,
Cambodia has returned to being a dozy enigma in a
world addicted to work. Its people, who once built
the mighty temple of Angkor Wat and 500 years
ago created vast irrigation systems in the delta of
the Mekong and then for no known reason
abandoned these structures to the encroaching
jungle, are today a lesson to us all. They have
rejected consuming and commuting in favour of
contemplation. They have stared into the abyss of
two horrendous opposing forms of human
exploitation and simply turned the clock back to
happy tranquil days of leisure. They have
discovered a new path which has led them back to
the soft contented life that existed long before Pol
Pot applied his terrifying yoke. The potential
Cambodian contribution to the idle revolution is
boundless. Here is a people who can convert latent
idlers by example and at the same time teach new
refinements in the art to the most proficient. The
Great Powers have all tried to get Cambodia

moving, to put its people to work, to impose discipline and generally get the place organised. All have failed. The French tried. The Americans attempted it. Even the Russians had a go through their support of the Vietnamese invasion but all to no avail. As soon as these bullies left, frustrated to insanity by the attempt, the Cambodians returned to type and continued their inert existence.

Everywhere you go in Cambodia you will hear their favourite phrase: "Up to you". It is difficult for the new arrival to understand the depths of the philosophy of "up to you" but is a concept every idler should adopt. It is one step on from the "Let's not and say we did" mentality which despite its bravado hides a smidgen of guilt. "Up to you" has no guilt attached. The words are applied to everything because no Cambodian would dream of imposing his, or more often her, wishes. It is always up to you. The spectrum of its use ranges from the purely practical – "Would you go to market for me?", "Up to you" – through the slightly confusing – "Do you smoke?", "Up to you" – to the completely baffling – "When is your baby due?", "Up to you". With this simple phrase the Cambodians themselves avoid deciding anything. Decisions mean responsibility and responsibility smacks of work and commitment and resolve. Cambodians will go to any lengths to avoid a

pronouncement for pronouncement is action of a sort and on the whole action is best avoided.

And it was ever so. Crossing from Vietnam in the early 1950s Norman Lewis observed: "the bamboos and the underbrush had gone, and with them the dark winged, purposeful butterflies of the Vietnamese forests. Here only trivial fritillaries fluttered over the white prairie grass. Great pied kingfishers as well as the large and small blue varieties encrusted the edges of yellow pools and ditches that served no economic purpose. There were no rice-fields. Cambodians lounge inertly about the rare villages... So far, the Grendel of colonial capitalism had been kept at bay. The Cambodians are practising Buddhists... (and this) has produced a tradition, a permanent state of mind, which makes its followers neither adept as exploiters nor amenable to exploitation. The Cambodians... are by their own design, poor, but supremely happy.... The Vietnamese, whose Buddhism is diluted almost the point of non-existence, has a competitive soul, is a respecter of work for its own sake, and strives to increase and multiply. As he will work hard for himself, he can be made to work hard for others, and is therefore the prey of the exploiter. Cambodians don't suffer from this affliction."

The encouraging thing about Cambodian idleness is that it covers the entire social spectrum. The Prime Minister learned that King Norodom Sihanouk had abdicated in favour of his ballet dancing son, Prince Norodom Sihamoni, by reading a message on the king's own website telling his indifferent people that he found the responsibilities of being head of state too irksome. Newspaper reporters based in Bangkok and Saigon (no busy correspondents here in Phnom Penh) dashed off uninformed articles that would have sat well on the pages of Evelyn Waugh's Scoop. "New king returns to tumultuous welcome in the streets...", "A proud and traditional nation looks forward under a new monarch...". All lies. Yes there was joy on the streets but this was because the coronation meant an extra three-day holiday in a month when there had been only five official festivals hitherto. I

have not met a single Cambodian that took the streets to see the coronation or even watched it on television. Knowing well the traditions of his people and despite having spent the last thirty five years dancing in Paris, King Sihamoni declared that the nation should continue to respect his outgoing father and keep both kings' birthdays as national holidays along with his mother's for good measure. The Cambodian's one regret is that despite his zest for life the 51 year old King Sihamoni has never married thereby denying his loyal subjects a holiday for his spouse's birthday. However he has promised to come back for Royal Ploughing Day every year.

At the other end of the spectrum lies, quite literally, Mr Chan. He is paid as my guard which is an anachronism in itself as the days of intruders and robbers passed with the disappearance of the United Nations (who tried to force a new constitution on the Cambodians). His hours are divided between three inactivities. As night watchman he sleeps in his hammock in a little wooden house in the best spot in my garden and his two day shifts are evenly divided between two armchairs strategically placed so that one is always in the shade on either side of the leafy road outside. He has two leisure activities. One is watching the brightly coloured fish that he has, without reference to me, installed in my main water tank and the other is to pick coconuts from the trees in my garden so that he can sell my fruit to his friends. In the days when the Vietnamese pushed out the Khmer Rouge Mr Chan joined the Russian Navy and served in the Black Sea fleet but on his return forgot his Russian and presumably his nautical skills and reverted to his energetic life of leisure. Just now he does it at my expense but he knows that he will have other paymasters who will be as easily manipulated as this one. My daughter asked him once why, with his family living in the same city, he wished to pass his hours in a hut in my garden. "Because my wife is small and ugly," was his mysterious reply.

For the office worker the day starts at the surprisingly early hour of seven o'clock but let me reassure you that one gathers at one's place of work simply to join colleagues for an hour of breakfast before knuckling down to a solid three and a half hours. This is followed by a two and a half hour break which involves another massive meal and a well-earned sleep. Then it is back to the office for as much as three hours in the afternoon although travelling time is taken out of office time not yours. If you live further away you are at your desk less and just in case you feel like spoiling the system with a little voluntary overtime doors are padlocked and the electricity switched off outside these official hours.

I was taken aback one afternoon to find a monk installed on the sofa in my office. With shaven head and saffron robes he was slumbering quietly when I returned from my lunchtime siesta and more bizarrely greeted me as an old friend asking informed questions about my work. After an hour it dawned on me that this religious sage was in fact my colleague Mr Sarim who, as he later explained, was obliged to fulfil spiritual obligations to his dead mother and so had become a monk for a day. It was in fact one of the last times I ever saw him in the office. Shortly after he rejected modernisation saying, "They are not lazy, these computers. They have to be working all the time." He then abandoned his desk for a smallholding that he created in the dusty car park where he bred peacocks. This compromise kept him on the payroll while allowing him to pursue his hobby. Cambodians are not much given to competition. One colleague turned down promotion and an increase in salary with the words, "Thank you, but I'd rather be the head of a chicken than the tail of an elephant."

General des Essars, who was in command of the French troops in Cambodia said that what he saw as "the trouble" was that the Cambodians lacked Western motives. How could he control a people whose aim in life was purely to acquire virtue, who saw no point in competitive endeavour? If they only bothered to gather possessions for the spiritual benefit of giving them away, why work hard? ☯

FILM:

MARLON BRANDO: THE METHOD & THE MADNESS

Paul Hamilton salutes Brando's noble efforts to escape relevance and embrace artistic redundancy

THE METHOD

"When strong, appear weak. Brave, appear fearful. Orderly, appear chaotic. Full, appear empty. Wise, appear foolish. Many, appear to be few. Advancing, appear to retreat. Moving quickly, appear to be slow. Taking, appear to leave. In one place, appear to be in another."

Wang Xi, from *The Art Of War* by Sun Tzu.

A nice, tidy Hollywood biopic ending for Marlon Brando would have been him dying after his revelatory work for *The Godfather* and *Last Tango In*

THE LAST TANGO IN PARIS

THE LAST TANGO IN PARIS

Paris, both made in 1972. But life isn't nice and tidy and Brando, Hollywood's most frustrating, untameable, contrary and volatile son, stuck around for another 32 years, his primary purpose seemingly to drive his most passionate supporters to face-hiding despair with yet another sickeningly overpaid and embarrassingly underplayed cameo role in a film of zero artistic merit. How could anyone reconcile the apparent hypocrisy of the man who baulked and railed against the star-maker machinery of Hollywood, the media meat-packing machine, the spiritual emptiness and capitalistic decadent Roman Empire squalor; who only found peace away from the saddening crowd on Native American reservations or his Pacific paradise Teti'aroa, who would then betray his principles and easily succumb to the lure of Big Bucks in the sure knowledge that the resulting work would only diminish his stature? An answer lay in Brando's assertion that his job was of little interest to him. *Last Tango In Paris* was his final, and finest, effort and he never again wished to exert himself so self-revealingly again. In his autobiography, *Songs My Mother Taught Me*, he admits that when *Tango* was finished, "I decided that I wasn't ever again going to destroy myself emotionally to make a movie. I felt I had violated my innermost self and didn't want to suffer like that that anymore. [... W]hen I've played parts that required me to suffer, I had to experience the suffering. You can't fake it. You have to find something within yourself that makes you feel pain, and you have to keep yourself in that mood throughout the day [...] You have to whip yourself into this state, remain in it, repeat it in take after take, then be told an hour later that you have to crank it up once more because the director forgot something."

Tango is more Brando's masterpiece than director Bernardo Bertolucci's for it is Brando's improvised and shockingly autobiographical dialogue – here, he is both physically and emotionally naked – rather than Bertolucci's conception that grabs and holds and twists and chokes. Bertolucci had devised a porn flick for the

> "I decided that I wasn't ever again going to destroy myself emotionally to make a movie"

intelligentsia, the basic plot being two complete strangers meeting in a vacant flat and fucking with no recourse to love or identity ("No names!" demands Brando's character, Paul. "I've been called a million names"). This is the type of scenario hornily scribbled out by the hairy of palm for a billion grumble mags. Also clichéd is the absolute distance in the protaganists' backgrounds: Jeanne (Maria Schneider) is barely in her twenties, with a happy loving relationship. She is vivacious, pouty, impetuous, open, honest, naïve, an unselfconscious butterfly just breaking free of her chrysalis, a freewheeling spirit. Paul is at the other, down, end of the seesaw – grey-haired and paunchy, he is an aged jade who has seen it all, done it all, ate, drank and fucked it all. He is in turmoil and freefall following his unfaithful wife's suicide. He is sour, dour, manic and panicked. He is a shadow

> "My father was a drunk... tough, whore-fucker, bar-fighter, super-masculine... My mother was very... very poetic... and also a drunk"

no expression of sexual desire but a rant of self-hate dredged up from the abyss. How far is Brando acting? How close is he to being himself? Like Brando, Paul has no respect for conformity ("All uniforms are bullshit") and is the son of alcoholics. He quietly opens up to Jeanne, "My father was a drunk... tough, whore-fucker, bar-fighter, super-masculine... My mother was very... very poetic... and also a drunk." In such moments, we feel like eavesdroppers more than paying viewers. He attains Stanislavsky's ideal of acting being a "public solitude".

Brando was possessed of a martyr complex and has suffered more ritual beatings in movies than any other "star". *The Wild One*, *On The Waterfront*, *Mutiny On The Bounty*, *The Chase* and on and on, and every time it's because he chose to stand outside of the herd and to reveal a feminine, caring face in a hard-hearted macho world. It's in his sole self-directed feature *One-Eyed Jacks* that his Christ and Oedipus obsessions become inseparable. As outlaw Kid Rio (a role he plays as a kind of parody of Elvis Presley), he is tied to a post – his arms outstretched in crucifixion style – and has his back whipped in the town square by Sheriff Dad Longworth. You don't have to hold a trunk of doctorates in Psychology to spot the subtle-as-a-flying-mallet allusion Brando's making of his relationship with his father.

In a sense, Marlon Brando was the world's oldest child. He retained a restless, insatiable curiosity about people, politics, nature and nurture, which fed back into his performances and gave them their intensity and power, but also burgeoned the belief that acting was a silly and unimportant job. A half-hour documentary filmed in 1965, *Meeting Marlon Brando*, fascinatingly captures all the sides of Brando in microcosm.

He is caught at a publicity launch for a film he has no interest in and the various reporters have not seen (although that doesn't prevent them from gushing how good the film is). Brando horses around with male interviewers, flirts outrageously with females, interviews a black woman about equality, and throughout he pays rapt attention to

under heavy blankets. As the doors of experience are opening wide for Jeanne, they have already slammed shut for Paul. What do they have in common other than the ability to fuck? For Jeanne the sex is novel, liberating, daring, fun. For Paul it's an exorcism, a manifestation of purging his soul of the poison of disenchantment and disappointment. Any claims that *Tango* is "erotic" are dispelled by Brando's journey to his personal heart of darkness. The promises of titillation are constantly undermined and subverted by Brando. When Jeanne masturbates on the mattress, Paul remains in an adjoining room, crouched down and examining a small table lamp. After considering it for a moment he begins to weep. He is desolate. Is he thinking of his dead wife – a light that's been extinguished? And again, as Jeanne fist-fucks him, he fantasises of her being forced to copulate with a dying pig. This is anyone in his eyeline. He's studying their dialects, their colloquialisms, their postures. He takes it all in and files it away for future reference. He disarmingly and effortlessly turns the tables and makes his inquisitors the centre of attraction.

What is missing from *Meet Marlon Brando* is his genius for scatology, a unique gift brought to the fore of Tango. He uses it in fun and in deep dark seriousness and always in an original manner. He is Lenny Bruce, Philip Larkin, Derek & Clive.

Paul's downfall is triggered by breaking his own rules to their game. He insisted at the outset there should be no names, no history, nothing outside the apartment to enter their abstract idyll, but Jeanne has brought him out of his shell, won him over, and now he wants to be part of her life in the outside world. He has fallen in love. She, however, has resolutely kept within the parameters and is determined that their dance come to an end. Paul tries without success to get her drunk in a hotel ballroom, affecting a Jack Hawkins-type English stiff upper lip accent akin to the one Brando would employ for *A Dry White Season* in 1989.

Tango climaxes with Jeanne shooting Paul dead on the bedroom balcony of her home. As he dies, Paul removes the bubblegum from his mouth and sticks it to the balcony railing. A perverse yet typically natural gesture by Brando, it is as mysterious as it is mundane. Is the bubblegum an emblem of the mess he's made of everything? Is it his way of leaving her a little forget-me-not?

THE TEA HOUSE OF
THE AUGUST MOON

Brando achieved a pinpoint clarity and insight to the (male) human condition with his performance – if indeed it is a "performance" since that word is redolent of putting on masks and adopting false attitudes – and created a living poem for the soul in *Last Tango In Paris*. Thereafter, he abandoned poetry and spent the rest of his time on the big screen improvising limericks and nursery rhymes. Ah, but what splendid, silly rhymes!

SUPERMAN

THE MADNESS

"Attack complete emptiness with complete fullness."

Cao Cao, from *The Art Of War* by Sun Tzu.

"Don't act. Behave!" was the motto of Stella Adler, Brando's drama teacher. Post-Tango, Brando amended her slogan to "Don't bother to act. Misbehave." Responsive to the child within himself, he crossed the borderline from Childlike (innocent, curious, delightful, playful) to Childish (petulant, restless, infuriating, ignorant). As a child bores of its toys, so Brando grew tired of acting. His subsequent performances are scarred by a deep-cut desire to expose and ridicule the mechanics of his craft, just as a child would dismantle a toy to discover how it works or to simply, malevolently, destroy it – preferably in the presence of the parent or relation who bought it, just for added spite. This is what Brando managed to get away with as soon as Hollywood decided he was big box office again. He would demand – like a spoilt brat – glutinous millions of dollars for a few weeks' work and then insist upon 11.3% of the gross takings. (The percentage, with its ludicrous "point three",

was a figure Brando made up on the spot in a moment of silliness. Even more silly was the film studios' capitulating to his whims.) Sick and tired of working for the machine, Brando seized his opportunity to gain the upper hand and had Hollywood doing his bidding. It can be argued that the vast amount of weight he piled on from the mid-1970s on was a deliberate act of defiance. By systematically destroying his good looks with discomfort eating he achieved self-ownership. His immense fatness rendered his iconic public image of sullen but sensitive beefcake invisible. Zen Buddhists believe that a work of art can be enhanced from a deliberate damaging. Marlon Brando had to break himself to find a kind of beauty within that perhaps only he alone could appreciate. In his perversely consistent adherence to improvising rather than doggedly sticking to the script he retained his air of being "in the moment", even if it meant highlighting the superficiality of everyone and everything around him.

Following Brando's four-year absence from the screen following *Tango* came the off-beat Jack Nicholson western *The Missouri Breaks*. Everything about the film is quite predictable until Brando's entrance thirty minutes in. Playing a regulator (a Wild West private detective-cum-mercenary) employed to drive away Nicholson's proto-hippy horse-rustlers from respectable farmsteaders, Brando subverts our suspensions of disbelief. When he first speaks it is in a cod-Oirish accent, a pastiche of Richard Harris at his most mellow. Later, for no reason, his Blarney Stone-swallowing tones are transformed to an English accent. What he speaks is barely coherent. The man talks in riddles, allusions, double-talk, mumbo-jumbo, cryptic metaphor. He is playing devious mind games. Brando also displays his penchant for mad headwear and disguise. Chinese coolie hats, bandanas, slave trader panamas adorn his head. The best costume is saved till last, when he kills a rustler whilst dressed in a granny's gingham dress, pinny and Easter bonnet. By going all out in the eccentricity stakes, Brando could have jeopardised the film. Instead he redeems it and gives it a uniquely surreal and menacing flavour. He wouldn't always be so lucky.

In 1978 he turned in a brief cameo in *Superman*, playing the eponymous hero's dad, Jor-El. In a moment of high camp Brando elected to sport a preposterous white bouffant syrup, looking for all the world like The Bee Gees' granddad. Not a moment of great dignity. Brando must have revelled in the damage to his reputation.

Brando's colleagues and collaborators have attested to his goofball humour and pranksterism. Perhaps his greatest prank was in *Apocalypse Now!* Not only had he neglected to research and build his character Kurtz, the American colonel-gone-loco in the Vietnamese jungle, he also hadn't

> Brando elected to sport a preposterous white bouffant syrup, looking for all the world like The Bee Gees grandad. Not a moment of great dignity

bothered to read either the script or the source novel, Joseph Conrad's *Heart Of Darkness*. Adding insult to injury, Brando informed director Francis Ford Coppola that he was unhappy about his weight and didn't want to be seen onscreen. The compromise reached was that Brando could play his role almost totally in shadow, his shaved head occasionally looming into dim light, and – rather than waste time learning lines – he would improvise and free-associate. This he did... interminably. The result was that, instead of Martin Sheen discovering at the river's end a devil in human form he found a fat, bald version of Peter Cook's park bench bore E.L. Wisty droning tediously on about "the horror". It's an act of wilful sabotage, Brando engineering the perfect anti-climax to Coppola's longwinded and pretentiously flatulent epic. A brilliant disaster.

BUY IDLER MUGS

Still
O N L Y
£4.99
+P&P

HOW TO ORDER YOUR IDLER MUG
(£4.99+£1.50p&p)

CALL THE IDLER MUG HOTLINE: 020 7691 0320 OR GO TO: WWW.IDLER.CO.UK

Fast forward some twenty years and one finds in the lamentably dull Johnny Depp vanity project *The Brave* some very strong clues as to how Brando could successfully have portrayed mad, bad Colonel Kurtz. Here he is, for all of eight minutes, playing the electric wheelchair-bound McCarthy, a producer of snuff movies. Johnny Depp's vapid Native American is offering himself up for video'd death sacrifice in order to get the $50,000 that will enable his family to break out of their penury. Brando's performance is edgy, adventurous, ambiguous, detailed. As he enters he momentarily loses control of his wheelchair – "Whoops!" – which instantly relays the fact that this is no cartoon villain. He is a fallible human. Like Paul in *Tango* and Lee Clayton in *Missouri Breaks*, McCarthy plays a plaintive melody on a harmonica – a way of soothing his soul. He wears his hair in a ponytail, garish lipstick across his mouth and sports a string tie. Like Rimbaud, he contains multitudes. McCarthy gasps when he sees the young and beautiful Depp and we sense his remorse at what card life dealt for him. Tenderly, thoughtfully, hesitantly, McCarthy ruminates on birth and death, and the necessity for pain in both and always in between. But is McCarthy speaking eloquently from the heart or is it a bogus act, a subtle show of hucksterism used many times before to sway the scared and undecided? We cannot be certain. Brando conjures a dark, magical spell of warm sympathy and cold terror. How typical that one of his great performances should be thrown away in a straight-to-DVD bore of a film. It lies in a shop somewhere, like treasure.

The Island Of Dr Moreau from 1996 could justifiably be cited as the nadir of all Brando's work – and, yes, the film stinks – but it is fascinating for putting all of Brando's cynicism, delinquency, madness and neurasthenia in full view. He takes the eccentricities from *The Missouri Breaks* and multiplies them a thousand-fold. Dr Moreau appears atop a Popemobile designed by Steptoe & Son to survey his "children" – mutant anthropomorphic results of his gene experiments. His face is painted white, his eyes are obscured by large sunglasses, his body by white robes. A flower power neck-chain hangs down his vast chest. With his set of protuberant choppers and his silly-ass English accent he is reminiscent of Michael Bentine (it's Marlon Brando's Potty Time!). Once again there's a bravura display of bonkers headwear, including a tin chimney which his daughter pours ice cubes into to cool his twittish brain. Brando deconstructs the art of acting to mere tomfoolery, the pastime of idiots. It's simply putting on mad clothes and stupid voices. *The Island Of Dr Moreau* is a million miles away from *Last Tango In Paris*. What Brando achieved – exhilaratingly – in Moreau is a spectacular public suicide, a negation of all he was and what he "represented". When Moreau is torn to bits by his children we hardly notice it. We certainly don't care. Brando expresses no shock, no fear in his being murdered. He is utterly passive, detached from the proceedings. Numb.

Marlon Brando showed us that the greatest thing anyone could do with a natural talent is to destroy it before it destroys you. What matters in the end is being true to your own inner vision no matter what the cost. And the rest of it? In his own immortal phrase, "It can take a flying fuck in a rolling donut." ◉

ELEVEN YEARS, 34 BACK ISSUES

1: August '93
SOLD OUT
Dr Johnson
Terence McKenna

2: Nov~Dec '93
SOLD OUT
Homer Simpson
Will Self

3: Jan~Feb '94
£8.00
Bertrand Russell
Charles Handy

4: April~May '94
SOLD OUT
Kurt Cobain
Matt Black

5: July~Aug '94
SOLD OUT
Douglas Coupland
Jerome K Jerome

6: Sept~Oct '94
SOLD OUT
Easy Listening
Richard Linklater

7: Dec~Jan '95
SOLD OUT
Sleep
Gilbert Shelton

8: Feb~Mar '95
SOLD OUT
Jeffrey Bernard
Robert Newman

9: May~June '95
SOLD OUT
Suzanne Moore
Positive Drinking

10: July~Aug '95
SOLD OUT
Damien Hirst
Will Self

11: Sept~Oct '95
£4.00
Keith Allen
Dole Life

12: Nov~Dec '95
£4.00
Bruce Robinson
All Night Garages

TO ORDER YOUR BACK ISSUES:

Go to www.idler.co.uk, or call 020 7691 0320 with your credit card, or make a cheque out to "The Idler" and send it to: The Idler, Studio 20, 24-28A Hatton Wall, London EC1N 8JH. You must include P&P cost as follows: P&P: Issues 1-24: 50p per issue. Issues 25-34: £2 per issue. T-shirts £1 per item. For European Community, add 50%. For Rest of World, add 100%

13: Jan~Feb '96
SOLD OUT
Stan Lee
Life As A Kid

14: Mar~Apr '96
£4.00
Bruce Reynolds
Will Self

15: May~Jun '96
SOLD OUT
Hashish Killers
Alex Chilton

16: Aug~Sept '96
SOLD OUT
John Michel
World Poker

17: Nov~Dec '96
SOLD OUT
John Cooper Clarke
Cary Grant

18: Spring '97
SOLD OUT
Thomas Pynchon
Ivan Illich

19: Summer '97
£4.00
Psychogeography
Henry Miller

20: Winter '97
SOLD OUT
Howard Marks
Kenny Kramer

21: Feb~March '98
£7.00
The Gambler
Bez

22: April~May '98
SOLD OUT
Alan Moore
Alex James

23: June~July '98
SOLD OUT
Summer Special
Tim Roth

24: Aug~Sep '98
SOLD OUT
Krazy Golf
David Soul

MAN'S RUIN 25: Winter 1999
£15
The first book-format Idler, featuring Louis Theroux's Sick Notes, Will Self, Howard Marks, Adam and Joe and Ken Kesey

PARADISE 26: Summer 2000
£5
Jonathan Coe meets David Nobbs, Nicholas Blincoe on Sherlock Holmes, Tiki Special, Iain Sinclair on the London Eye

THE FOOL 27: Winter 2000
£5
Village Idiots, World Of Pain, Arthur Smith's diary, The Big Quit, James Jarvis's World of Pain, John Lloyd

RETREAT 28: Summer 2001
£10
Louis Theroux meets Bill Oddie, Jonathan Ross meets Alan Moore, Alex James meets Patrick Moore, plus Andrew Loog Oldham

HELL 29: Winter 2001
£10
Crass founder Penny Rimbaud, Crap Jobs Special, Boredom Section, New fiction from Niall Griffiths, Mark Manning, Billy Childish

LOVE 30: Summer 2002
£10
Louis Theroux meets Colin Wilson, Johnny Ball on Descartes, Crap Towns, Devon Retreat, Chris Yates interview, Marchesa Casati

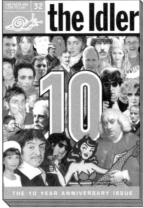

REVOLUTION 31:
Winter 2002
£10
Dave Stewart, Black Panthers,
Saint Monday, Allotments, Riots,
Introducing the Practical Idler
section

ANNIVERSARY 32:
Winter 2003
£10
Damien Hirst on why cunts sell
shit to fools; Marc Bolan; the
pleasures of the top deck; Walt
Whitman; happiness

LADIES OF LEISURE 33:
Spring 2004
£10
Clare Pollard is sick of shopping;
Girls on bass; the wit and
wisdom of Quentin Crisp;
Barbara Ehrenreich

THE FOOD ISSUE 34:
Winter 2004
£10
Joan Bakewell on life
as a freelancer; Bill
Drummond's
soup adventure;
The Giro
Playboy;
Falconry; why
supermarkets
are evil and
Jerome K
Jerome

TO ORDER:
CALL:
020 7691 0320
OR VISIT:
www.idler.co.uk

THE VIEW FROM THE SOFA

Greg Rowland's in dreamland

CHRIS WATSON

If you watch enough TV, eventually all your wishes will come true. For many years I had wished for a TV show that would bring the disparate worlds of Ufology and double entendre together. Then, one night, cast in the deft shadows of crepuscular creep, my dreams were answered by Astra, the Pagan Goddess of Satellite Telly.

It was a special on Sky One, all about a UFO phenomenon called *Rods*. My excitement superseded even the hyperbole of a 1970s Marvel Comics cover – this was the double entendre "slug-fest of the century".

The Rods themselves are shiny lines only visible in photographs or sloweddown videos. Rod enthusiasts opined about the possible threat from this fast-moving alien lifeform. Of course, threequarters of the way through the show, a beardless man (all Rod enthusiasts have *Joy Of Sex* beards) quietly mentioned that these Rod effects were just birds catching the light in an unusual way. Yet that didn't stop the fun. We were thus treated to the joyous phrases I breathlessly recount to you here.

"You can take a picture of your own Rod," invited the American announcer, full of delicious promise.

"That's my Rod! That's my Rod!" exclaimed the hysterically excited bearded Rod Researcher while watching a sloweddown video playback.

"Could this be the world's biggest Rod?" asked the announcer while showing a "rod" darting in and out of a tornado in a somewhat suggestive manner.

"Something flashed by my daughter while she was playing in the garden. Only when I slowed down the video did I realise that it was actually a large Rod," said a concerned parent from Arkansas.

Yet, amidst my snuffling smutty smirks, I was struck by a deep melancholy. Could the singularly British appreciation of the double entendre be doomed to the dustbin of history? I fear that the twin "prongs" of HIV-awareness and the liberalisation of education may be the "chopper" which cuts down the "bush" of British smut. We Britains are now taught that sex is something to be discussed with frankness and honesty. This process goes against those centuries of folk culture that cited sex as naughty, dirty, shameful and extremely funny.

We must all stand "firm" therefore against the tide of cleanliness that threatens our finest cultural export! For our children's sake we must preserve the culture of double entendre for the generations to come, I do not want to be the last man in England, who sniggers at the mention of the word "helmet". For Knob's Sake, remember the children! ☺